I WILL NOT BE SHAKEN

A Songwriter's Journey Through the Psalms

I WILL NOT BE SHAKEN

A Songwriter's Journey Through the Psalms

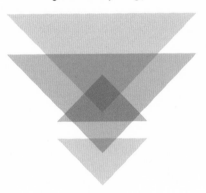

JAMIE HOWISON | STEVE BELL

SIGNPOST MUSIC

Winnipeg, Manitoba

I Will Not Be Shaken: A Songwriter's Journey Through the Psalms

Published by Signpost Music
1578 Erin Street | Winnipeg, Manitoba | R3E 2T1
Phone: 1-800-854-3499
Email: office@signpostmusic.com
www.signpostmusic.com

Written by Jamie Howison and Steve Bell
Foreword by Gordon Matties
Copy editing by Kelly Milne
Project management by Amy Knight
Cover design by Roberta Hansen
Administration and all-around support by Faye Hall & Dave Zeglinski

Printed and bound in Canada by Friesens Printing, Altona, Manitoba

Library and Archives Canada Cataloguing in Publication

Howison, Jamie, author
    I will not be shaken : a songwriter's journey through the Psalms / Jamie Howison and Steve Bell ; foreword by Gordon Matties.

Includes bibliographical references.
ISBN 978-0-9683048-5-3 (pbk.)

    1. Bible. Psalms--Criticism, interpretation, etc. 2. Bible. Psalms. Selections--Paraphrases, English. I. Bell, Steve, 1960-, author II. Title.

BS1430.52.H69 2015   223'.206   C2015-902351-3

CONTENTS

ACKNOWLEDGEMENTS

JAMIE

I would like to acknowledge my indebtedness to Robert Farrar Capon (1925-2013), with whom I shared two days of great conversation just as the ideas for this book were beginning to percolate.

Also Alfred Bell, who has had such a clear influence on Steve, but who also provided me wise and psalmic guidance at a particularly thorny point in my pastoral ministry.

STEVE

I wish to thank my manager Dave Zeglinski, and our staff Faye Hall and Amy Knight who care for the many behind the scenes details of this work. In particular, Amy Knight carefully shepherded the production of this book.

JAMIE AND STEVE

We wish to thank Gordon Matties for reading the manuscript, attending to the music, and beautifully writing the book's foreword.

We are also grateful our wives, Catherine Pate and Nanci-Lynne Bell for lovingly sharing the life we live that makes this work possible.

FOREWORD
Gordon Matties

My wife and I took Steve Bell's *Comfort My People* along with us to Jerusalem on my sabbatical in 1991-92. We must have listened to that cassette tape until we wore it out. We were so profoundly nourished by that album that we wrote to Steve and asked him when he might put out a second album. We could hardly wait. Steve gave us a gift that hasn't worn out in nearly a quarter century since.

Comfort My People included the first three psalm settings that Steve wrote, and they are the first three songs in this collection. Over the years I have hoped that Steve would put out a separate psalms collection; I am thrilled that the project has now come together. Jamie Howison's interpretive insights, combined with Steve's storytelling, make this resource both a guidebook to Steve's musical offerings and a handbook for our own engagement with the Psalms.

I've taught a Psalms course off and on for thirty years. I've begun every class session by playing a musical setting of a psalm. Although I have more than a dozen CDs of psalm settings, I've always begun by looking for an appropriate setting among my collection of Steve Bell CDs. Now we have all his psalm songs on one CD.

Here are several observations about this collection. First, Steve's psalm settings do what psalm settings should: they set the psalm to music. But, unlike all my other psalm CDs, which for the most part include musical settings of entire psalm texts, Steve's songs reflect a wrestling with and an embodiment of the psalm. Each of these songs (and the accompanying stories) testifies to a patient waiting with a psalm, an immersion in and a wrestling with a psalm, or a receptive opening to the gift that a psalm might be offering.

Second, Steve's psalm-songs emerge from a grappling with his own life experiences. His encounters with people, his wonder at the beauty of God's good earth, his experiences of divine silence, and perhaps with his own inner demons (if I might use that word in a more secular sense here) are the birthing materials out of which the creative offering emerges. There is no abstract "preachiness" in these psalm-songs apart from their embodiment in the struggle, joy, pain, frustration, and hope that comes—whether asked for or not.

Third, the songs reflect a journey into and out of the Psalms. Sometimes through the journey inward, a psalm gives birth to music. At other times through the journey outward, music is the child of the encounter with a psalm. Sometimes the music rushes out and overwhelms. Sometimes a psalm invites long gestation. Sometimes a dream explodes into song and a psalm-song emerges out of darkness. Through Steve's song-stories we learn that one cannot presume on either the Psalms or on the music. They speak, they comfort, they challenge, they inspire. But the music is servant, rather than master, of the work of attending to the psalm. In that respect these psalm-songs testify to a spirituality for the long haul. They do not offer a quick fix even though at times a psalm may speak to one's situation in remarkable ways.

Above all these songs are not simply "settings" of the Psalms. They are, rather, engaged "readings"—vulnerable meditations on how the Psalms have read Steve Bell. They are "renditions," or even Midrash—the result of a decades-long immersion in the Psalms, which has produced artistic extensions of the Psalms that have become psalms in and of themselves. The Psalms are often springboards to new poetic artistry, both in word and music. Steve draws inspiration from a psalm, and in so doing takes us both into the psalm in fresh ways, and draws us further along the trajectory initiated by the psalm.

I have no doubt that by attending to these songs, and by reading Jamie and Steve's accompanying reflections and stories, those familiar with Steve's music will discover themselves drawn deeper and further into the Psalms themselves. Those hearing Steve's music for the first time in this collection will, I hope, be drawn to his other recordings and will discover how the spirituality of the Psalms also infuses everything else he does.

Gordon Matties is Professor of Biblical & Theological Studies at Canadian Mennonite University in Winnipeg, Manitoba, Canada

DEAR READER

You'll notice the order of the psalm-song reflections in this book are not sequential. Rather, they are in the order that Steve wrote them, and so the order itself is somewhat biographical.

Each chapter begins with a psalm, followed by Jamie Howison's reflection. At the end of each chapter is a brief note from Steve explaining a bit about the process, or circumstances behind his rendering, followed by the lyrics he wrote.

Each chapter, of course, corresponds to the music you'll find on the Psalms Collection CD by Steve Bell. If you don't already have a copy, you can purchase albums at www.stevebell.com or download from iTunes.

The book and CD can be used together as a helpful resource for personal or small group reflection.

INTRODUCTION

This project has been slowly simmering for years. We had our first conversation about doing a shared book on these psalm-based songs back in 2004, and in fact the earliest drafts of many of these reflection pieces were written over the course of that winter. For various reasons, we decided we needed to put this project on the proverbial back burner, though from time to time we'd revisit the idea to see if maybe we might turn up the heat and get it really cooking. In the end it seems as if the slow simmer was what this book really needed; and so, eleven years on, we've reached the place where we can finally add some extra seasoning and share what we've produced.

And truthfully, long before we even talked about writing this sort of book, we were laying its groundwork. From the beginnings of our friendship in 1989, we've been having long and lively conversations about theology, life, music, books, ideas, and the Psalms; somehow the Psalms made their way into almost every one of our conversations.

We share the experience of finding in the Psalms a language and a framework for prayer, for worship, and for speaking of God in a searching and open way. We've both experienced the authenticity and immediacy of these ancient spiritual resources as a kind of liberation of the self from selfish or overly self-driven concerns and perspectives. Yes, a good number of these songs and prayers do fit the category of personal psalms, written in the first-person singular. Yes, a fair number do seem to strike strong notes of something akin to self-pity, even self-righteousness. Yet for all the times they may begin there, the psalms rarely leave off in that space. Again and again, these extraordinary poems and songs of personal and corporate experience reflect a movement from the *merely* personal or the *merely* human into the deeply relational; relationship to God and relationships lived within the horizon that is the abiding presence of God.

In Steve's case, engaging the Psalms was a big part of what

13

"unlocked" him as a young songwriter, though he is certainly not the first artist or thinker or pray-er to have experienced their liberating power. We think here of Bono, lead singer for the rock band U2. In his very fine introduction to the Grove Press Pocket Canon's *Selections from the Book of Psalms*, Bono has much to say about the potency of the Psalter.

> Words and music did for me what solid, even rigorous, religious argument could never do—they introduced me to God, not belief in God, more an experiential sense of GOD. Over art, literature, reason, the way to my spirit was a combination of words and music. As a result the Book of Psalms always felt open to me and led me to the poetry of Ecclesiastes, the Song of Solomon, the book of John... My religion could not be a fiction but it had to transcend facts.[1]

"My religion... had to transcend facts," which is the very thing the Psalms call out to us. While they are often transparent in their confession of sin, and in many places powerfully celebrative of the story of faith, the Psalms are not confessional statements. They are also not guides to correct theological thinking, and they certainly do not constitute a handbook for releasing somewhat self-absorbed, young songwriters from writer's block. They are ancient scripts for engagement with God. Ancient, yet somehow one of the most contemporary resources people from every age have been able to lay hands on.

This is why in his introduction to the Psalms in *The Message*, Eugene Peterson can speak of these ancient hymns and prayers as being the single greatest resource for those who struggle to pray.

> My usual response when presented with these difficulties is to put the Psalms in a person's hand and say, "Go home and pray these. You've got wrong ideas about prayer; the praying you find in these Psalms will dispel the wrong ideas and introduce you to the real

---

[1] Bono, "Introduction," *The Pocket Canon Psalms* (New York: Grove Press, 1999), p. ix.

thing." A common response of those who do what I ask is surprise—they don't expect this kind of thing in the Bible. And then I express surprise at their surprise: "Did you think these would be the prayers of *nice* people? Did you think the psalmists' language would be polished and polite?"[2]

Peterson can rightly see the Psalter as something of a school of prayer, and that is largely because it is not a technical handbook. This is not about technique at all, but rather about honest speech and deeply authentic resources. They speak to us now, across thousands of years, precisely because those writers dared to speak truthfully.

And so it is that the theologian and writer Robert Farrar Capon, having spent the year of his 77th birthday facing serious and discouraging health issues, could say:

> I've read the Psalms like mad over the years. And
> I've had all the reactions everyone has had: glorious,
> problematic, difficult, nasty and snotty and vengeful
> and just weird. And also totally applicable to me at this
> point: "forsake me not in my old age."[3]

And so it is that the great German theologian Dietrich Bonhoeffer could write from his prison cell that the Psalms "helped to preserve me from any serious spiritual trial."[4]

> (Prayer in time of trouble) is always a difficult matter,
> though our misgivings about it can hardly be good. In
> Psalm 50 we are told quite clearly: "Call upon me in the
> time of trouble: so will I hear thee and thou shalt praise
> me." The story of Israel is one long story of such cries
> for help.[5]

---

[2] Eugene Peterson, *The Message* (Colorado Springs: Navpress, 2002), p. 910.
[3] Robert Farrar Capon, unpublished personal interview. Shelter Island, New York, January 14, 2004.
[4] Dietrich Bonhoeffer, *Letters and Papers from Prison* p. 40.
[5] *ibid.,* p. 66.

The list of testimonials could go on and on, stretching to include quotations from St. Benedict and Martin Luther, Thomas Merton and C.S. Lewis. We could easily produce a psalmic version of a good old-fashioned tent revival meeting, but as is true of that tradition, not *everyone* needs to testify every time...

What exactly are the Psalms? They have tended to be received in one of two ways, and only rarely been given a well-rounded and balanced treatment. Either they have been received as devotional material for individual and corporate use, or they have been the subjects of scholarly—and too often arid—study. The tradition has long identified them as the "Psalms of David," in spite of the fact that the Hebrew text attributes them to a variety of authors ("the Korahites," Asaph, Solomon, even Moses) alongside of David. There is a large body of scholarship that even suggests none actually come from David's hand, yet their association with David as a crowning, archetypal figure in the story of Israel is unavoidable. With seventy-three of the psalms dedicated in David's name, including thirteen that directly reference a very specific event in David's life, the Lutheran biblical scholar James Limburg makes the observation that while our English translations read, 'A Psalm of David,' "the Hebrew can be translated as 'for David' or 'to David.' Therefore the heading could mean the psalm was written by David, indicating authorship, but it could also mean that the psalm was written *for* David or was dedicated *to* David." In the case of Psalm 3, the dedication reads "A Psalm of David, when he fled from his son Absalom," which in Limburg's view might well mean something like, "This is the sort of prayer David prayed, when his life was in extreme danger."[6] We can never know for sure, of course, but one way or the other, as the glorious, raw, fallen, and oh-so-human centrepiece of Israel's self-understanding, David simply *is* connected to the spirituality of the Psalms.[7]

What is widely agreed upon in the scholarly literature is that the

---

[6] James Limburg, Psalms (Louisville, KY: Westminster John Knox Press, 2000), p. 8.

[7] Bono's approach might be helpful: "But to get back to David, it is not clear how many, if any, of these psalms David or his son Solomon really wrote. Some scholars suggest the royals never dampened their nibs and there was a host of Holy Ghost writers... Who cares? I didn't buy Leiber and Stoller... they were just his songwriters... I bought Elvis." *The Pocket Canon Psalms, p.* xii.

book of Psalms, as we currently know it, is the product of the Babylonian Exile and of the subsequent rebuilding of the temple in Jerusalem. When Judah's leading lights were taken away to the prison ghettos of Babylon (leaving behind a dispirited Jerusalem that would, in 587 BCE, be razed to the ground, temple and all), they were faced with a set of deep problems:

> Has our God lost, and been shown to be weak and defeated?

> With no temple to focus us and no palace to defend us, is it even possible to worship this God?

> In a strange and alien land, how will our faith be preserved, enlivened and transmitted?

In short, "how can we sing the Lord's song in a foreign land?" Turn to Psalm 137, and work with us here, to see how this well-known psalm of exile encapsulates—and answers—its own question. It is by the rivers of Babylon where these people find themselves, weeping in remembrance of the hope and promise of what was. It is there where the captors—the soldiers and the ghetto police— ask for the exiles to share one of their "songs of Zion"; one of the songs that celebrates the glories of Jerusalem, after the manner of Psalms 46 and 84. And yet doesn't Jerusalem lie in ruins? Their demand for such a song must have come across as something like, "hey Jew-boy... sing us one of your songs about that city of yours we've just destroyed... dance, boy, dance!" It is as humiliating as when a much later generation of Jewish musicians was made to play in orchestras in Nazi concentration camps, or when the great African-American blues legend Lead Belly was coerced into playing for upscale Manhattan cocktail parties wearing prison garb and a decorative ball and chain. No... we won't sing. We will hang our harps up on the branches of the trees, and vow ourselves to silence. And then follows the truly disturbing verses 7 through 9, in which the captives dream of revenge. "Happy shall they be who take your little ones and dash them against the rock!"

We have to wrestle here with two things. Firstly, if any of us had seen and experienced the violence and humiliation experienced by this community, would we have felt less violence welling up in our own souls? The integrity of Psalm 137 lies in its rawness, and in its willingness to take that rawness to the very throne of heaven. Secondly, how does the writer express his vow of silence and his loss of lyric voice? By writing a song. The singing of the song becomes deeply subversive, in that songs will not be sung for the oppressor, but resistance will be sung nonetheless. The writer here shows us that the real question has become "how can we *not* sing the Lord's song in this strange land?" To *not* sing is to forget, and for exiles the most dangerous thing is forgetfulness.

These songs of resistance are collected with the older songs the exiles had brought with them, and are shared in homes and around community circles as a way of exploring and establishing identity in a foreign place. Churches in our day, increasingly out of step with the dominant culture, would do well to attend to this experience.

There is broad scholarly agreement that the book of Psalms as we know it became the working hymn book of what is known as "Second Temple Judaism." Back at home after the exile, with the long slow process of rebuilding in view, the collection was solidified. And it was solidified in all of its familiar variety and messiness. Praise, lament, anger, and consolation. Individual and corporate. Dare to say it all, and ask God to carry us in all of our seasons. We find that to be an extraordinarily courageous approach to prayer.

———

Over the years, we've both been deeply influenced by the writings of the Old Testament scholar Walter Brueggemann, freely sharing with each other his many books, articles, and sermons. Working with both the scholarly literature and the lived experience of the church, Brueggemann proposes "that our life of faith consists in moving with God in terms of,
   a. being securely *oriented,*
   b. being painfully *disoriented,* and
   c. being surprisingly *reoriented.*"[8]

———

[8] Walter Brueggemann, *Praying the Psalms* (Winona, Minnesota: Saint Mary's Press, Christian Brothers Publications, 1993), p. 14.

Life holds these seasons, and because the Psalms are borne of lives lived and of a willingness to speak the truth, the Psalms align with these seasons as well, and so can be viewed in terms of psalms of orientation, psalms of disorientation, and psalms of new orientation. Brueggemann works with this schematic grid in a number of books and articles, most helpfully in his little book, *Spirituality of the Psalms.*[9]

The psalms of orientation reflect a perspective of safety and trust, "a sure sense of God's orderliness [which] is not always [a] high and noble faith."[10] Verging on a sort of *status quo* faith, what might be offered as prayers of affirmation and celebration can easily sound smug and uncritical. Think, for instance of these lines from Psalm 37:

> I have been young, and now am old,
> yet I have not seen the righteous forsaken
> or their children begging bread.
> (Psalm 37:25)

Does this imply that people who walk with experiences of being forsaken or abandoned in life are unrighteous, or that those children whose lives are marked by hunger are the offspring of unrighteous, and therefore undeserving, families? We don't believe that this is what the author of Psalm 37 is attempting to say, but you can see how selective reading of such verses in isolation could be problematic. Besides, if you have never really been hungry or destitute, it is very easy to become smug.

The psalms of disorientation tell of the undoing of any such smugness, and of the experience that "Life is savagely marked by incoherence, a loss of balance, and unrelieved asymmetry."[11] This is the stuff of being very much "in process"—the expressions that arise when a person is in a state of disorientation: laments, dreams

---

[9] Walter Brueggemann, *Spirituality of the Psalms* (Minneapolis: Fortress Press, 2002).

[10] *ibid.,* p. 20.

[11] *ibid.,* p. 25.

of revenge, bleak doubt. Whatever resolution is offered is so often in terms of a resolute and challenging cry to God to *do something*. Psalm 137 is a prime example of this type.

Reorientation is the surprise we know (or believe or desperately hope...) is on the horizon. Reorientation is always by grace through faith, and never just a personal therapeutic advance.

Rather the speaker and the community of faith are often surprised by grace, when there emerges in present life a new possibility that is inexplicable, neither derived nor extrapolated, but wrought by the inscrutable power and goodness of God.[12]

This is not just a case of coming full circle, because, "the psalmists know that we can never go home again."[13] Reorientation may well recapitulate something from the older, safer place of secure orientation, but it is from a place of having experienced a gracious and oftentimes difficult re-creation. Think here of the story of Jacob wrestling with the angel (Gen. 32:22-32). He has met the same God he encountered earlier in his dream of the ladder to heaven (Gen. 28:10-17), yet in his night of wrestling, Jacob is re-created in and through God. Yet Jacob's reorientation is also a wounding, and so he limps for the rest of his newly reoriented life.

In all of the seasons of life, the Psalms speak the truth. In a society which so often wants us to deny the truth of what is really going on, this is a liberating and awe-filled resource for life. "Poets exist so the dead may vote," writes Elie Wiesel.[14] The Psalms exist so that those votes can be cast again and again in our lives.

And the votes are not just cast in the formation of *my* thinking or *my* personal prayer. A large number of the psalms are communal, with roots in the shared liturgical life of ancient communities. Yet even the individual and personal psalms are not to be thought of as coming from outside of the shared faith and life of the people of God. The faith of the individual *is* the faith of the community, and the agonizing doubt or despair of the individual implicates

---

[12] *ibid.*, p. 47.
[13] *ibid.*, p. 47.
[14] Elie Wiesel, cited in *ibid.*, p. xiv.

the entire community.

When church communities choose to sing or say only the "nice bits," we do ourselves a great disservice. In much of contemporary Western Christianity, praise and worship is our primary corporate language, and we render ourselves mute by such a limiting vocabulary. "Such worship," claims Brueggemann, "is destructive because it requires persons to engage in enormous denial and pretense about how life really is."[15] To have resources in our hands that dare to break the silence and name the truth is a great gift. Speaking the truth of our story, we have taken the first step toward relinquishing any pretense of idolatrous control over the smooth running of our lives. It is all given to God.

A brief aside on the psalms of vengeance. As we have suggested in our comments on Psalm 137, vengeful and even poisonous anger is quite understandable at particular points in our individual and collective experiences. If we experience something that evokes such powerful emotion, we should take it to God in prayer... regardless of the orthodoxy or politeness of our expression. "God behaves in the Psalms in ways he is not allowed to behave in systematic theology," writes the Benedictine Sebastian Moore;[16] and I'd venture to say that the people of God are invited to voice that which falls outside of any tidy systematic lines. The God met in the Psalms can cope with everything we can possibly say or feel or fear.

Further, as Brueggemann emphasizes in *Praying the Psalms*, in the Christian scriptures we have to contend with the proclamation that, "God has wrought [justice and vengeance] upon God, and so the world has been purged and grace has triumphed."[17] It is only after an honest acceptance and expression of all that we are and all that we feel, then, "our rage and indignation (can) be yielded to

[15] Walter Brueggemann in Beth LaNeel Tanner, "How Long, O Lord! Will Your People Suffer in Silence Forever?" in Stephen Breck Reid, ed. *Psalms and Practice* (Collegeville, MN: The Liturgical Press, A Michael Glazier Book, 2001), p. 144.

[16] Sebastian Moore, in Kathleen Norris, *The Psalms* (New York: Riverhead Books, 1997), p. vii.

[17] Brueggemann, *Praying the Psalms,* p. 68.

the mercy of God. In taking this route through the Psalms, we take the route God has gone. We are not permitted a cheaper, easier, more 'enlightened' way."[18] It was precisely these insights from Brueggemann that allowed Steve to complete his song, "Somebody's Gotta Pay" (*Waiting for Aidan*, 2001), written to express his rage over the sexual victimization of his then 13-year-old foster daughter. In the life, death, and resurrection of Jesus Christ, God *has* reconciled all things, but it was no easy or cheap sleight of hand that wrought that reconciliation. While we remain on this side of the fully realized Kingdom of God, we should have no expectation that our own smaller reconciliations—with our enemies, our injured loved ones, our own mortality and death—will come without cost; without rage or doubt or just plain bewilderment.

One final set of comments on translation will complete our introduction. Unless you happen to be able to read Hebrew, you will always be at arm's length from the original text. One of the primary concerns at work in many standard English translations of the Bible is the preservation of the poetic and lyric nature of the original Hebrew. And yet sometimes a free translation like Eugene Peterson's *The Message* can alert or even jar the reader into a fresh appreciation of these ancient texts. Peterson set out to produce quite a stark translation of contemporary idiom, and within that goal has been very successful. Consider, for instance, Peterson's rendering of the opening verse of Psalm 51:

> Generous in love – God, give me grace!
> Huge in mercy – wipe out my bad record.

How very different from the more conventional translation offered in the New Revised Standard Version:

> Have mercy on me, O God,
> according to your steadfast love;
> according to your abundant mercy
> blot out my transgressions.

---

[18] *ibid.*, p. 68.

Although we sometimes find the psalms in *The Message* to be a bit flat and contemporary, there are times when this disarmingly unexpected version can do a very particular sort of work on us.

In a different way, the same can be said for the use of much older translations, such as the King James Version. Of this version, the writer Kathleen Norris comments, "Despite the archaic grammar, the King James packs more emotional punch—more resonance, both musically, in one's ear, and inwardly, in one's soul."[19]

We made the decision to include in this book another classic English translation; one marked by the same sort of archaic grammar as the King James, and with the same "emotional punch." Myles Coverdale's sixteenth century translation of the Psalter is incorporated into the English *Book of Common Prayer*, and is widely regarded as a literary masterpiece. Alongside the King James Version of the Bible, the works of Shakespeare, and the *Book of Common Prayer* itself, it is a landmark in the development of the modern English language. In the opinion of Hebrew Bible scholar Walter Deller, "for poetic grip, you can't beat Coverdale," and this praise is in spite of the fact that Coverdale was working not from the Hebrew original but from the Latin Vulgate. His translation is at once poetic and spiritually charged; and while borne of a world very different from our own—Coverdale can't even begin to imagine such things as gender-inclusive language, for instance— its aims are really not that far from our own. This is the translation of the Psalms that was prayed by generation after generation of poets: from George Herbert and John Donne to Christina Rossetti, T.S. Eliot, and W.H. Auden; and for this reason alone we should pay attention. Considering also how this translation has been used liturgically in common prayer for over 450 years, and given our own commitments to shared and common worship, that is hardly insignificant.

For the purposes of this book, we've used the Coverdale translation at the beginning of each chapter, where the corresponding Psalm is written out in its entirety. Within Jamie's reflection pieces

---

[19] Kathleen Norris, *The Psalms*, p. xx.

themselves, all references are from the New Revised Standard Version (NRSV).

We hope that this project might play some role in calling you—and us—to an ever deeper and more truthful life in the presence of God. But then again, where else could we be but in the presence of God?

> Whither shall I go then from thy Spirit:
> or whither shall I go then from thy presence?
> If I climb up into heaven, thou art there:
> if I go down to hell, thou art there also.
> If I take the wings of the morning:
> and remain in the uttermost parts of the sea;
> Even there also shall thy hand lead me:
> and thy right hand shall hold me.
> (Psalm 139:6-10, *Book of Common Prayer*)

"Bidden or unbidden, God is present."[20]

Jamie Howison and Steve Bell
Lent, 2015

---

[20] A saying attributed to Desiderius Erasmus, 16th Century.

LORD, thou hast been our refuge: from one generation to another. Before the mountains were brought forth, or ever the earth and the world were made: thou art God from everlasting, and world without end. Thou turnest man to destruction: again thou sayest, Come again, ye children of men.

For a thousand years in thy sight are but as yesterday: seeing that is past as a watch in the night. As soon as thou scatterest them they are even as a sleep: and fade away suddenly like the grass. In the morning it is green, and groweth up: but in the evening it is cut down, dried up, and withered.

For we consume away in thy displeasure: and are afraid at thy wrathful indignation. Thou hast set our misdeeds before thee: and our secret sins in the light of thy countenance. For when thou art angry all our days are gone: we bring our years to an end, as it were a tale that is told. The days of our age are threescore years and ten; and though men be so strong that they come to fourscore years: yet is their strength then but labour and sorrow; so soon passeth it away, and we are gone.

But who regardeth the power of thy wrath: for even thereafter as a man feareth, so is thy displeasure. So teach us to number our days: that we may apply our hearts unto wisdom.

Turn thee again, O Lord, at the last: and be gracious unto thy servants. O satisfy us with thy mercy, and that soon: so shall we rejoice and be glad all the days of our life. Comfort us again now after the time that thou hast plagued us: and for the years wherein we have suffered adversity. Show thy servants thy work: and their children thy glory.

And the glorious majesty of the Lord our God be upon us: prosper thou the work of our hands upon us, O prosper thou our handywork.

PSALM 90

JAMIE HOWISON

With a bold and courageous truthfulness the psalmist
tackles the problem of the relationship between God
and man from the point of view of God's eternal being
and man's transient nature, and, taking his faith
unflinchingly seriously, pursues this problem to its
uttermost depths so that the words of this psalm never
fail to appeal irresistibly to men's hearts. Here a man
with the mature experience of old age looks back upon
human life and against the background of the eternal
being of God apprehends its nature and its ultimate
coherence. And in so doing he enters upon the way
which alone leads from man's denial of life to the true
life, that is, to a confident affirmation of life as rooted in
God himself.21

Artur Weiser's observation that it is "a man with the mature
experience of old age" whose voice is in evidence in Psalm 90

---

[21] Artur Weiser, *The Psalms* (Philadelphia: The Westminster Press, 1962), p.
595.

is striking. That this is the only psalm attributed to Moses—an attribution widely believed to be a later addition to the text[22]—is notable. For all the acclaim that David is the great hero of Israel and the figure most powerfully associated with the Psalms—"the Elvis of the Bible" as U2's Bono would have it[23]—this psalm is received as one that must have come from the hand and heart of Israel's earlier and greatest hero, Moses. To be sure, the psalms associated with David are often penetrating, truthful, and disarming; but Psalm 90 penetrates and disarms in its truthfulness.

Verse 1 proclaims the truth on which the whole psalm is built:

> Lord, you have been our dwelling-place
> in all generations.
> (Psalm 90:1)

This is a particularly interesting and ironic proclamation in a psalm attributed to Moses, who led a pilgrim people to the very edge of the promised "dwelling place," but who never himself actually crossed over. The singers of these words knew that the "dwelling place" was always more than simple geography, and that it was often in the midst of displacement in desert or in exile where the people found themselves most aware of their "place" within the care of their God.

Verses 2 through 6 emphasize the eternal and changeless nature of God's being.

> Before the mountains were brought forth,
> or ever you had formed the earth and the world,
> from everlasting to everlasting you are God.
> (Psalm 90:2)

As they speak of the transcendence of God, these verses also begin to say something about the transience and fragility of human life. Mortal life is like a "dream" or like "grass" (v. 5), both of which

---

[22] *Ibid,* p. 595.
[23] Bono, "Introduction," *The Pocket Canon Psalms* (New York: Grove Press, 1999), p. x.

come and go with the passing of day and night.

Yet there is more than the truth of the divine power and timelessness to divide humans from God. Humanity is mired in sin, and this sin is seen as the cause of anger in the heart of God. This psalm depicts how sin deepens our frailty and hastens our demise:

> For we are consumed by your anger;
> by your wrath we are overwhelmed.
> You have set our iniquities before you,
> our secret sins in the light of your countenance.
> For all our days pass away under your wrath;
> our years come to an end like a sigh.
> The days of our life are seventy years,
> or perhaps eighty, if we are strong;
> even then their span is only toil and trouble;
> they are soon gone, and we fly away.
> (Psalm 90:7-10)

Having faced up to the truth of our sinfulness, the psalmist can now pray a prayer of mature and seasoned hopefulness:

> So teach us to count our days
> that we may gain a wise heart.
> (Psalm 90:12)

This single phrase launches the closing section of the psalm, in which the writer looks for a deeper balancing of human life within the depths of the divine presence. A prayer for gladness and satisfaction, it is unafraid to use the word "prosper" or "establish." Yet unlike the shallow "prosperity gospel" of certain current church circles, it asks,

> Let the favour of the Lord our God be upon us,
> and prosper for us the work of our hands—
> O prosper the work of our hands!
> (Psalm 90:17)

"Prosper the work of *our* hands." But note that, at the heart of this prayer lies the appeal, "Not my will, but yours be done" (Luke 22:42b). Not *my* prosperity, but that which is from the hand of God.

Steve's setting for his song is built around the closing section of the psalm, verses 13-17. There is a nod to verses 1-2 ("Lord for us you have been a refuge from age to age"), but there is no other substantial reference to the verses that precede the closing section. While Steve maintains a strong sense of the disconnect between God's eternal being and human frailty and dependence, this song does not take on the issue of *sinful* frailty. The question of sin goes unasked, perhaps because the song was written in 1989, before Steve had reached his 30th birthday. Here Weiser's comments about Psalm 90 being an expression of a "mature experience of old age" are germane. Were Steve to turn his attention to a Psalm 90-inspired song now, with over two decades of additional life experience under his belt, would he find himself wrestling just a bit more thoroughly with verses 7-11? I suspect he might. This is, after all, the artist who included the song "Eventide" on his 2001 CD *Waiting for Aidan:*

> For with much wisdom
> Comes much sorrow
> So the more that I know
> The more sorrow grows
> Like a fish caught cruelly
> Like a bird in a snare
> We are caught and we are captive
> Unexpectedly here

Still, Psalm 90 calls us beyond the bleak mood of the writer of Ecclesiastes, from which "Eventide" draws its inspiration. The mood of Ecclesiastes, in fact, needs to be drawn into conversation with the wisdom of Psalm 90. In the space between Steve's "Psalm 90" and his "Eventide," there is perhaps another song waiting to be written; a song that knows on a deeper level some things about age and wisdom and sin and hope—knows, in fact, that some things are simply given us.

> So teach us to count our days
> that we may gain a wise heart.
> (Psalm 90:12)

STEVE BELL

This is the first piece of scripture I set to music. It was written shortly after leaving the bar scene in the late 1980s. I was in my late twenties, married with two children, and beginning to realize I had no skills or training that would land me a decent job. I was quite worried about the future and feeling wretched and ashamed for having "wasted" a decade of my life in the clubs with nothing to show for it.

With no other options obvious to us, Nanci went back to work as a teacher (which she was quite happy to do) and I stayed home for a year with the kids (which I was less enthused about). Sometime that winter, having sunk into a mire of depression, I stumbled upon this psalm. I remember the words overwhelming me and tears flowing as a melody began to form. It never occurred to me that the song I wrote later that night was at once a desperate prayer for meaningful work, while at the same time an answer to that prayer, and the beginning of a lifelong vocation.

Psalm 90
music and lyric adaptation by Steve Bell

> Satisfy us in the morning with your love
> Satisfy us in the morning with your love
> That we may sing for joy
> And be glad in all our days
> Satisfy us in the morning with your love
>
> Match the days Lord, of our sorrow with your joy
> Match the days Lord, of our sorrow with your joy
> May your deeds be always known
> To the ones you call your own
> Match the days Lord, of our sorrow with your joy
>
> *May the favour of the Lord*
> *Rest upon us and our land*
> *And establish for us all*

The work of our hands
Yes, the work of our hands

Lord, for us, you have been our refuge from age to age
Lord, for us, you have been our refuge from age to age
Before the mountains were formed
And the earth and the world brought forth
You are the everlasting Lord

PSALM 23

THE LORD is my shepherd: therefore can I lack nothing. He shall feed me in a green pasture: and lead me forth beside the waters of comfort. He shall convert my soul: and bring me forth in the paths of righteousness, for his Name's sake.

Yea, though I walk through the valley of the shadow of death, I will fear no evil: for thou art with me; thy rod and thy staff comfort me.

Thou shalt prepare a table before me against them that trouble me: thou hast anointed my head with oil, and my cup shall be full. But thy loving-kindness and mercy shall follow me all the days of my life: and I will dwell in the house of the Lord for ever.

PSALM 23
SHEPHERD OF LIFE

JAMIE HOWISON

Without question, one of the most well known and highly sentimentalized of all the Psalms, the 23rd is counted by Walter Brueggemann as one of the "psalms of new orientation." This is perhaps ironic, because this psalm is so often used to express or evoke some feeling of overall confidence and pastoral comfort. It is widely requested for funerals, often by grieving families who have relatively marginal connections to the community of faith. References to the shepherd, green pastures, the valley of the shadow of death, and to dwelling in the Lord's house, all seem to make this the psalm d'jour for such occasions.

I say there is an irony here because, for all of its pastoral prettiness, the psalm also has a quality of resilient, almost rugged faith. The language is evocative, but what it finally evokes is a sense of the steadfastness of faith in a God who is faithful *even in the darkness.* To turn once again to Brueggemann,

> The reason the darkness may be faced and lived in is
> that even in the darkness, there is One to address. The

One to address is in the darkness but is not simply a
part of the darkness (John 1:1-5). Because the One has
promised to be in the darkness with us, we find the
darkness strangely transformed, not by the power of
easy light, but by the power of relentless solidarity.[24]

This is precisely what the psalmist knows, such that whether in
green pasture or darkest valley, there is trust in that solidarity.
Remember: here the banquet table is set even in the presence of
enemies, which is not an expected image produced by a writer
who is still reorienting his faith.

Which leads me to recall a story from a time in my life and ministry
that can only be described as one of deep disorientation. A former
pastor of the parish I was ministering in had been brought up on
a series of criminal charges related to the sexual molestation of a
dozen complainants. The parish community found itself wrestling
with very difficult and painful questions. The fact that he had been
gone from the community for more than a dozen years (having
been dismissed from active ministry due to an earlier conviction)
hardly removed the sting, as we now had to face the reality that
one of our own had been a serial offender. Add to this situation the
general rule that "trauma triggers trauma," and these were hard
days indeed.

I contacted Steve's father, Dr. Alf Bell, to arrange a conversation.
Alf has extensive experience and expertise working with convicted
sexual offenders, and was the ideal resource for sorting out pastoral
strategies. We met for lunch in a quiet restaurant and spent
the first forty-five minutes going over some of the literature on
working through such issues. At the end of a very helpful, though
largely theoretical conversation, Alf pushed back from the table
and began to speak of my personal need for spiritual resources.

"I know that some people find writers like John of the Cross to be
great spiritual helps, but I always turn to the Psalms. I particularly
like the 23rd Psalm, which I think comes right out of David's
experience as a shepherd. Why don't you just close your eyes,

---

[24] Walter Brueggemann, *Spirituality of the Psalms,* p. xiii.

Jamie, and let me talk to you about this psalm." And so right there in that restaurant, I closed my eyes and began to listen.

"Imagine yourself as one of the lambs, living with the flock in good green pasture land, with fresh clear water in the nearby stream. Life is good there, and the shepherd is your guarantee of safety.

"Weeks pass, though, and you notice that the grass is drying and the stream is becoming muddy and warm. The rains aren't falling, and things aren't quite so good. The grass is prickly in your mouth, and the water fails to quench your thirst. And one day, the shepherd gets up, takes staff in hand, and begins to move the flock. Up the hills you all move, higher and higher toward a mountain pass. The climb is steep, and you begin to lose your enthusiasm for this life. A couple of times you lag behind the flock, and when you do the shepherd is there to push you on with his staff. When you are so tired and you don't even know where you're headed, that staff against your flank just hurts.

"By the time you reach the pass, it has become dark. The fading sunlight is lost behind the high rock walls, and it is cold and miserable. Tired and despondent, you lie down, thinking it might be better to just stay there and die.

"It is at this point that an old sheep comes over to talk to you. He has made this trek before. He knows that on the other side of the pass is another valley, and in that other valley the grass will be better and the spring-fed stream will be running. He has learned that this shepherd knows what he's doing, and that the prods and pushes of his staff are expressions of that knowing.

"The old sheep speaks only two simple sentences. 'I've done this before; keep moving.' And then, 'Just stay close to the shepherd.'"

There was a long pause, and I slowly opened my eyes. Alf's eyes were dancing with light. "I'm the old sheep, Jamie. Just stay close to the shepherd."

All through that challenging time, colleagues would ask if I was seeing a counsellor, or if I had a spiritual director. "No," I would say, "I've got something better. I've got an old sheep."

STEVE BELL

One lazy afternoon, while noodling around on my guitar, I stumbled on a bluesy riff that intrigued me; it quickly developed into a fully formed melody, but without any lyrics.

I remember Nanci walking past and saying, "That's different for you. What's it about?"

I had no idea.

For the next few weeks I kept returning to the song but couldn't come up with any ideas for a lyric. It was kind-of bluesy, kind-of country, kind-of sensual... was it to be a lament? a love song? a story? I didn't know.

Then one night, while laying in bed only half awake, I suddenly and involuntarily sat bolt upright, startling Nanci out of her sleep.

"Psalm 23!" I blurted out.

"What do you mean Psalm 23?" she asked, a little annoyed for the rude awakening.

"That song I'm writing... it's Psalm 23."

I don't remember exactly what she said in response, but she was pretty sure that I should just go back to sleep, which I did.

The next morning I woke up wondering if the previous night's episode had only been a dream. I slipped out of bed and stole downstairs where I opened up several different Bible translations to the famous psalm. Within minutes the lyrics fell together like pieces of a magic puzzle that came to life when completed.

Shepherd of Life
music and lyric adaptation by Steve Bell

The Lord of life is my shepherd
He leads me with nothing to want
And he leads me along
With his staff and his rod
He is here, to comfort my fears

Though I walk through the valley
I walk with his hand in mine
Thought I passed my last breath
In the shadows of death
But I'm still here safe on the other side

Here with the water beside
Cool in the grasses I lie
Here with my Lord
Who gently restores
He's the shepherd of life

There's a table laid out before me
There's a cup in which joy overflows
Surely goodness and love
Will follow me all of the days...
All the days of my life

PSALM 126

WHEN THE LORD turned again the captivity of Sion: then were we like unto them that dream. Then was our mouth filled with laughter: and our tongue with joy. Then said they among the heathen: The Lord hath done great things for them.

Yea, the Lord hath done great things for us already: whereof we rejoice. Turn our captivity, O Lord: as the rivers in the south.

They that sow in tears: shall reap in joy. He that now goeth on his way weeping, and beareth forth good seed: shall doubtless come again with joy, and bring his sheaves with him.

PSALM 126
THE LORD HAS DONE GREAT THINGS

JAMIE HOWISON

Psalm 126 is part of a small collection of psalms (120-134), all of which carry the title "A Song of Ascents." Biblical scholars and translators are not of one mind as to what this title signifies. Martin Luther, for instance, understood it to be a musical instruction akin to what is found in certain other psalms—"To the leader: with stringed instruments" (Psalm 67)—and so translated it as "A song for the higher choir."[25] Lawrence Toombs, picking up on the fact that the original Hebrew word relates to both "staircase" and "pilgrimage," suggests that pilgrims on the Jerusalem temple stairway quite probably sang them liturgically.[26] Artur Weiser, on the other hand, renders the title as "A Pilgrim Song," picking up on the pilgrimage setting but suggesting a less formal liturgical usage than Toombs.[27] This latter position is held by a fair number of

---

[25] Artur Weiser, *The Psalms* (Philadelphia: The Westminster Press, 1962), p. 100.
[26] Lawrence E. Toombs, "The Psalms" in Charles M. Laymon, *The Interpreter's One-Volume Commentary on the Bible* (Nashville: Abingdon Press, 1971), p. 260.
[27] Weiser, p. 741ff.

scholars, and suggests that for the Jews of the Diaspora (the Jews scattered well beyond the borders of Israel thanks to war and exile, and later, to trade and commerce), these psalms were the "road songs" for the long and arduous journey "home" to Jerusalem.

Following this line, it is hard not to hear in Psalm 126 strong echoes from Israel's experience of the Babylonian Exile and subsequent journey home.

> When the Lord restored the fortunes of Zion
> we were like those who dream.

When the Lord took us home and rebuilt us in our city, it was like the end of the nightmare of the prison ghettos of Babylon.

> Then our mouth was full of laughter,
> and our tongue with shouts of joy;

We sang and danced and wept in the streets.

> Then it was said among the nations,
> 'The Lord has done great things for them.'
> The Lord has done great things for us,
> and we rejoiced.

Yes, we danced at this liberation; liberation wrought by God alone, and not by freedom fighters or an allied army. The nations, with their kings and soldiers, just shake their heads in wonder at how this has come about.

> Restore our fortunes, O Lord,
> like the watercourses in the Negeb.

But the restoration has just begun. We're home, Lord, yet our city and our temple are still rubble. It looks impossible, but you, Lord, can make fresh water rush through barren deserts.[28]Restore us!

---

[28] Weiser writes, "... the congregation expect from their God nothing less than absolute miracle – rivers in the sun-scorched desert in the south, an impossible thought indeed!" p. 761.

May those who sow in tears
reap with shouts of joy.
Those who go out weeping,
bearing the seed for sowing,
shall come home with shouts of joy,
carrying their sheaves.

May those who knew only the hell of exile—those who packed bags of seed-grain on their backs to take with them into Babylon—may they come home with a rich harvest of grain and joy and laughter.

Regardless of whether or not Psalm 126 was written with the exile quite so directly in view, a nation whose imagination had been so thoroughly formed around the experience of exile and restoration could hardly have failed to hear and feel such references. Further, diaspora Jews fifty or even five hundred years later would have experienced their own Jerusalem pilgrimages as echoes of that first return and restoration. Surely those families traveling from Nazareth to Jerusalem for Passover (Luke 2:41) felt something of the deeper promise as they sang these words on the road. Did they sing this song with just a hint of subversive edge, holding out the dream that someday soon Jerusalem would be freed from her Roman occupiers?

When Steve sits with his guitar on the stage of a church or concert hall and asks, "Does anyone here like bluegrass?" is he not inviting us to partake in the stubborn and resilient hopefulness of a faith that knows the Lord has done—and will do—great things? Whatever tune and instrumentation was used by the first singers of this psalm, I like to think it might have been the ancient world's version of bluegrass: a little loose, open to variation and vocal playfulness, earthy and human and liable to get your feet moving, almost in spite of yourself. That sense of movement is so crucial to this traveling psalm, and it is a big part of why (Steve's song aside) it has such appeal. After all, as Christians we are people who find ourselves, in one way or another, most often out on the road.

STEVE BELL

Nanci and I belonged to an intentional church community in the early 1980s. Initially we met in the basement of a house in Winnipeg's Wolseley district. The group grew quickly, but instead of investing in a larger facility to meet in, we eventually divided into three groups: one stayed in the original location, another (which Nanci and I joined) moved into Winnipeg's inner city, and the third moved to a rural farm to live their common life on the land. The three groups regularly came together to worship, share stories and nurture relationships. On one such occasion, the rural group was sharing about their life and their struggles to be faithful stewards of the land in an age of high-yield farming, which often uses destructive practices. Someone read Psalm 126, which is rich with agricultural images.

As quickly as the psalm was read, I heard an accompanying melody and realized I was being gifted with a song. It took every ounce of concentration to keep the melody in my head until the gathering was over and I could get home to record it on my ghetto blaster. About a week later, feeling the song needed some polishing, I played it for songwriting friends Byron O'Donnell and Larry Campbell. Byron quickly came up with a soaring counter melody over the chorus, which we soon realized was the prime melody. Larry offered several significant improvements as well, and the song was born.

At the time I wrote this song I was listening incessantly to Emmy Lou Harris' *Angel Band* album, which was a collection of traditional gospel bluegrass songs. The influence is pretty obvious.

The Lord Has Done Great Things
music and lyric adaptation by Steve Bell,
Byron O'Donnell and Larry Campbell

> When the Lord brought out the captives
> When he set the prisoners free
> It was just like in a dream

And our mouths were filled with laughter
And our tongues with songs to sing
It was just like in a dream

And it was said among the nations
That the Lord had done great things

O the Lord has done great things
Filled our hearts with songs to sing
O the Lord has surely done great things

Restore to us our fortunes Lord
Give life to dying streams
Fill our hearts with songs to sing
For those who sow in tears
With only songs of joy will reap
Fill our hearts with songs to sing

And it is said among the nations
That the Lord has done great things

O the Lord...

For those who go out weeping
Carrying heavy bags of seed
There's a joy that harvest brings
They will come back singing songs of joy
And bearing golden sheaves
There's a joy that harvest brings

And it is said among the nations
That the Lord has done great things

O the Lord...

GIVE THE KING thy judgements, O God: and thy righteousness unto the King's son. Then shall he judge thy people according unto right: and defend the poor. The mountains also shall bring peace: and the little hills righteousness unto the people. He shall keep the simple folk by their right: defend the children of the poor, and punish the wrong-doer.

They shall fear thee, as long as the sun and moon endureth: from one generation to another. He shall come down like the rain into a fleece of wool: even as the drops that water the earth. In his time shall the righteous flourish: yea, and abundance of peace, so long as the moon endureth.

His dominion shall be also from the one sea to the other: and from the flood unto the world's end. They that dwell in the wilderness shall kneel before him: his enemies shall lick the dust. The kings of Tharsis and of the isles shall give presents: the kings of Arabia and Saba shall bring gifts. All kings shall fall down before him: all nations shall do him service. For he shall deliver the poor when he crieth: the needy also, and him that hath no helper. He shall be favourable to the simple and needy: and shall preserve the souls of the poor. He shall deliver their souls from falsehood and wrong: and dear shall their blood be in his sight.

He shall live, and unto him shall be given of the gold of Arabia: prayer shall be made ever unto him, and daily shall he be praised. There shall be an heap of corn in the earth, high upon the hills: his fruit shall shake like Libanus, and shall be green in the city like grass upon the earth. His Name shall endure for ever; his Name shall remain under the sun among the posterities: which shall be blessed through him; and all the heathen shall praise him.

Blessed be the Lord God, even the God of Israel: which only doeth wondrous things; And blessed be the Name of his majesty for ever: and all the earth shall be filled with his majesty. Amen, Amen.

PSALM 131

LORD, I AM not high-minded: I have no proud looks. I do not exercise myself in great matters: which are too high for me. But I refrain my soul, and keep it low, like as a child that is weaned from his mother: yea, my soul is even as a weaned child. O Israel, trust in the Lord: from this time forth for evermore.

PSALM 72 & 131
AS LONG AS THE SUN

JAMIE HOWISON

I have a very vivid memory of sitting with Steve in a North End Winnipeg coffee shop, listening as he struggled with the words of a song he had just recorded. He recited these lines from the chorus of that song:

> As long as the sun
> As long as the moon
> His justice shall reign
> And ever endure
> And there shall be peace...

He stopped the recitation, and said something to the effect that, "I sometimes find it hard to sing that. Where is the justice and peace right now in this world? How can I sing, 'for as long as the sun and moon endure,' when this world knows no peace?"

We went on to have a conversation about the power of proclaiming something that is, in the eyes of the world, just plain foolishness; which is not a bad sort of conversation to have, but... All these years later, I am finally ready to attempt a more thorough answer.

First of all, it is significant that this song has melded verses from two different psalms. Steve and his co-writer Larry Campbell have taken the poet's prerogative and reshaped some of the original material into a new form. What should be noticed, though, is that in this new form the material from Psalm 72 has been given substantially new textures.

The superscription to Psalm 72 attributes it to Solomon, and it reads as a prayer by Solomon for his own kingship. It is cast in the third person singular, such that the king prays "may he judge" or "may he live," with the "he" meaning himself. Listen, then, to the force of the verses that lie behind Steve's song:

> May he (the king) live while the sun endures,
> and as long as the moon, throughout all generations.
> May he be like rain that falls on the mown grass,
> like showers that water the earth.
> In his days may righteousness flourish
> and peace abound until the moon is no more.
> (Psalm 72:5-7)

This psalm now reads as a royal prayer for God to bless the monarch as an instrument of the divine will.

> As a result of the shower of the monarch's benevolence, equity and peace will bud and blossom until the end of time and universal sovereignty will vanquish all rivals. In effect, the monarch's dominion is as vast as God's, whose agent he is on earth.[29]

This is an enormously hopeful vision of what God might wring from the royal house. It is a vision borne of Brueggemann's category of "safe orientation." The crown having been passed from David—the shining, flawed, yet so beloved hero of Israel—to

---

[29] Konrad Schaefer OSB, *Psalms; Berit Olam:* Studies in Hebrew Narrative and Poetry (Collegeville, MN: A Michael Glassier Book published by The Liturgical Press, 2001), p. 72.

Solomon—the royal son with the reputation for great wisdom—all seems to set things up for a kind of golden age.

But things did not—and do not—pan out in the hoped for way. Solomon was a mixed blessing (see particularly 1 Kings 11:1-40), even more than his complicated and very human father. A prayer for a king's life to be linked poetically with the reign of sun and moon can become an implicit defense of the *status quo* and a form of social control.[30] Yet this prayer can also become a voice of social criticism, whereby the hopeful vision is a measuring stick against which the reality of a less than ideal monarch is measured. Ultimately—and this is the turn I believe Steve has made—it becomes a hopeful song of anticipation for a true kingship; the kingship of Messiah, of God, and—to make the move that a Christian *can* and *must* make—of Jesus the Christ. It is a kingship inaugurated ("the kingdom of God is within/amongst you"), yet still awaiting its culmination and fulfillment ("*maranatha* –come, Lord Jesus!"). It is a kingdom whose citizens dare to sing "as long as the sun," knowing full well the inability of any human ruler to offer such a reign. Knowing full well, too, despite all evidence to the contrary, such a reign is already in our midst. Reclaimed in such a way, this psalm does indeed tell us what is really going on.

The blending of Psalm 72 with Psalm 131 is significant. Brueggemann counts Psalm 131 amongst the "Psalms of safe orientation," but I am not entirely convinced. As Konrad Schaefer notes, this psalm begins with a perspective articulated in "three negatives, with a fourth one understood—*not* lifted up, *not* raised too high, *not* occupied in things too great (nor) in things beyond me."[31] He goes on to ask, "why would a prayer begin so emphatically with a denial, unless the opposite were suspect?"[32] This psalm reads to me like a prayer that could only be sung by someone who, in pride and preoccupation, had encountered some deep crisis of disorientation, and had then done the hard work of learning a security analogous to that of a child safe in a mother's arms. It is significant to realize that the original Hebrew

---

30   Walter Brueggemann, *Spirituality of the Psalms,* p. 20.

31   Schaefer, p. 312, italics added.

32   *ibid.,* p 312.

text indicates an image not of a nursing baby but of a weaned child. A weaned child—in this context perhaps two or three years of age—is old enough to begin to explore and encounter the world. This is a picture of a toddler, who *knows* that warmth and security are found in the mother's arms. He or she can have all things set right in mommy's lap: a scraped knee, hurt feelings, a nightmare ghost lurking in the closet... all can be healed in that place of consolation. Significantly, Psalm 131 identifies the God whom Jesus called Father, or Abba, with the mother of this vulnerable toddler.

As Steve and Larry have constructed this song, it becomes a call to trust even in the midst of a world in which we wonder if the sun and moon have darkened (Mk. 13:24); a world in which the call to live *now* as citizens of the kingdom is as pressing as when Jesus first challenged his followers to take that path. What at first seems like an all too optimistic royal psalm becomes, in this light, a song that sings of both our dream and our need for consolation in the arms of God. The reality is that the Christian life is lived in this tension.

STEVE BELL

I wrote this song at a time when there was a particularly acute crisis of hunger in Africa and the daily news was filled with images of decimated landscapes and wasting bodies. One night I had a dream that I was sitting in an enormous room. There were hundreds of thousands of people sitting cross-legged on the floor, each wrapped in a warm blanket, as the air was cool. What light there was had the effect of a flickering fire, although there was no visible source. God, a large old man, was sitting in the middle of the crowd and I was quietly sitting in his lap—not because I was special, but because it was my turn.

All were silent for the longest time, simply enjoying the quiet presence of each other, when suddenly an Ethiopian man stood awkwardly, and with great and sorrowful tears, he spoke about the famine that was ravishing his people and his land. When he was finished, he remained standing, awaiting a response from God who simply nodded an acknowledgment and kept silent.

Then, a woman stood to her feet. In vain she attempted to suppress her gut-wrenching grief as she spoke to God about her son who was lost in a drug addiction, and who would not likely survive without divine help. Again, God nodded but kept silent, and the woman eventually sat down.

Then, one by one, others stood up to speak about various sorrows, or terrors, each beseeching God to intervene. Each time God nodded but kept silent.

I started to squirm, feeling uncomfortable with the anger that was building in me in response to God's seeming indifference.

After several heart breaking petitions, all fell silent again—but now the coziness of the gathering was gone, and there was a menacing sense of betrayal building in the room. I looked up into God's face, searching for any sign of a heart that might break as ours were. I noticed water beginning to rim around his eyes until a tear formed and fell from his face to splash on mine. And then we all heard his soundless voice, not in our ears, but pressed upon our souls: "If you knew what I knew, you'd just sit."

This song followed from that dream:

As Long as the Sun
music by Steve Bell,
lyric adaptation by Steve Bell and Larry Campbell

My heart is not proud
And neither my eyes, O Lord
I'll not be concerned
With mysteries of life that are yet untold
But I am still
And quiet is my soul
Like a child whose mother holds
Yes I am still
And just like a child is my soul

For as long as the sun
As long as the moon
His justice shall reign
And cover the earth
And ever endure
And there shall be peace
From sea to sea
For as long as the sun
As long as the moon
Continue to be

Creation will bring
The good fruit of righteousness
My Lord will defend
And nations will call him blessed
So I am still
And quiet is my soul
Like a child whose mother holds
Yes I am still
For Israel's hope is the Lord

PSALM 13

HOW long wilt thou forget me, O Lord, for ever: how long wilt thou
hide thy face from me? How long shall I seek counsel in my soul, and
be so vexed in my heart: how long shall mine enemies
triumph over me?

Consider, and hear me, O Lord my God: lighten mine eyes, that I
sleep not in death. Lest mine enemy say, I have prevailed against
him: for if I be cast down, they that trouble me will rejoice at it. But
my trust is in thy mercy: and my heart is joyful in thy salvation. I will
sing of the Lord, because he hath dealt so lovingly with me: yea, I
will praise the Name of the Lord most Highest.

PSALM 13
HOW LONG

JAMIE HOWISON

Picture if you will, an evening at church. As I sit in those few quiet moments before people begin to arrive for worship, I find myself in deep and wordless prayer, aware that I am "weary and carrying heavy burdens" (Matthew 11:28). No one thing in particular is weighing on me, just a combination of the stuff of ministry, family, relationships, and life. I am all set to preach on the Lucan beatitudes (Luke 6:20ff.), in which Jesus proclaims blessing upon people who, for reasons of poverty or hunger or sorrow or rejection, know that they live in need: "blessed are you when you've bottomed out, such that you can no longer kid yourself into believing that you are a self-sufficient, self-providing master of your own life." This is at least part of what is going on in those odd blessings and corresponding "woes." It is great news, of course, to discover that you don't have to be—in fact can't be—that strong, because grace is sufficiently, abundantly and freely given by a wildly indiscriminate and loving God.

As people begin to arrive, I break my stillness and go to offer greetings. One person after another has stories to tell of weariness and burdens too heavy to bear. "You know how I've said before that we'd had the week from hell?" one woman asks me. "Well, *this* was the week from hell."

As worship begins, I am aware how Jesus' blessing of those who weep is particularly potent and immediate for us—for me—this night. But then another voice begins to ring from deep within my imagination: "How long?" I mean really, Lord, I think we get it here. The woman agonizing over her teenaged son, the family wrestling against terminal cancer, the person in deep conflict with a roommate, the wife whose marriage has just been punctuated by a big question mark; surely, all of us could stand to have a shot at grace without first having to face these tears.

> How long, O Lord? Will you forget me for ever?
> How long will you hide your face from me?
> How long must I bear pain in my soul,
> and have sorrow in my heart all day long?
> How long shall my enemy be exalted over me?
> (Psalm 13:1-2)

How about a direct, miraculous intervention here, Lord? Maybe just this once you could change the heart of the teenager, zap the cancer, make the roommate more reasonable, and the marriage partner easier to love. Maybe this time your blessed grace could be a bit more aggressive. We know our need, already...

"These psalms are the voices of those who find their circumstances dangerously, and not just inconveniently, changed. And they do not like it."[33] The psalmist dislikes this dangerous dislocation at least as much as I do, or anyone else in our hurting congregation for that matter. The psalmist even tries to leverage God with a bit of shame-based pressure, crying for divine intervention:

> Consider and answer me, O Lord my God!
> Give light to my eyes, or I will sleep the sleep of death,
> and my enemy will say, 'I have prevailed';

---

[33] Walter Brueggemann, *Spirituality of the Psalms* (Minneapolis: Fortress Press, 2002). p. 38.

> my foes will rejoice because I am shaken.
> (Psalm 13:3-4)

After all, what kind of God would allow this to happen to one of the faithful? Yet as Brueggemann points out, "It is the function of these songs to enable, require, and legitimate the complete rejection of the old (safe) orientation. That old arrangement is seen, if not as fraud, at least as inadequate to the new circumstance."[34]

So yes, the quick fix zapping would be nice, but it would not do a whole lot to deepen us into the reality of the changed circumstance. It would not do a whole lot to grow a people who can actually take on new life. "Costly grace," was Bonhoeffer's paradoxical phrase, which in this instance seems to have something to do with the formation of a people who manage to keep moving deeper and deeper into the gift, regardless of the cost.

The psalmist manages to resolve this lament by affirming that, just as trust has been offered before, so will rejoicing come again. "I *will* sing to the Lord," which means I *will* rejoice again "because God has dealt bountifully with me."

> But I trusted in your steadfast love;
> my heart shall rejoice in your salvation.
> I will sing to the Lord,
> because he has dealt bountifully with me.
> (Psalm 13:5-6)

These verses offer memory and stubborn resolution in one movement, and as such are a profoundly hopeful and faithful proclamation. Yet "how long?" is not a question far from the psalmist's mind. Neither is it far from my mind. Not today. Not ever.

---

[34] *Ibid*, p. 39.

STEVE BELL

My grandparents on my father's side were missionaries in China, which is where my dad and his siblings were born. I grew up hearing wondrous stories of adventure, sacrifice and profound faith. As wonderful as those stories were, however, they worked on me like a poison. For even though, since my earliest memories, I have felt destined for ministry, I have also felt myself too weak, fearful, doubtful and sinful to ever be of much service to God (at least the type of service everyone around me seemed to be in). I had too little faith, and too weak a character and spiritual constitution to rise to the calling. It was a shame I mostly accepted and carried.

Then, in my twenties, my disappointment in myself turned into disappointment in God. Although I never would have voiced it, I began to collect my disappointments in a pile: the prayers for my mother's healing that went unanswered (she has suffered from an anxiety disorder for much of her life); the prayers for deliverance from my own vices and doubts that went unanswered; the many times I had begged God for help in the uncertain early years of marriage and child rearing that appeared to go unanswered; and the time (as silly as it now seems) when I broke my arm, was in excruciating pain, and begged God for relief that didn't come. But the most profound disappointment of all was the unanswered request for a sense of God's nearness that others reported, but which I didn't experience.

Then I heard a sermon on Psalm 13. The psalm was described as a complaint to God, about God. It staggered me. I didn't know this could be an acceptable prayer. This song followed... as did the beginning of an adult prayer life.

How Long
music and lyric adaptation by Steve Bell

> How long
> Have you forgotten me oh lord
> How long

Hmmm....
Will you hide your face from me
How long
Look on me
Answer my call
Oh Lord my God
I need some light before I fall

How long
Will I wrestle with my thoughts
How long
Hmmm...
Must I have sorrow in my heart
How long
Look on me
Answer my call
I cry every night
But you don't seem to hear at all

Yet I'll trust in your love
Yes your unfailing love
And I will sing out my days
That you've been good to me
Yes you've been good to me

How long
Have you forgotten me oh Lord
How long
Hmmm...
Will you hide your face from me
How long
How long

I WAITED patiently for the Lord: and he inclined unto me, and heard my calling. He brought me also out of the horrible pit, out of the mire and clay: and set my feet upon the rock, and ordered my goings. And he hath put a new song in my mouth: even a thanksgiving unto our God. Many shall see it, and fear: and shall put their trust in the Lord.

Blessed is the man that hath set his hope in the Lord: and turned not unto the proud, and to such as go about with lies. O Lord my God, great are the wondrous works which thou hast done, like as be also thy thoughts which are to us-ward: and yet there is no man that ordereth them unto thee: If I should declare them, and speak of them: they should be more than I am able to express.

Sacrifice and meat-offering thou wouldest not: but mine ears hast thou opened. Burnt-offerings, and sacrifice for sin, hast thou not required: then said I, Lo, I come, In the volume of the book it is written of me, that I should fulfil thy will, O my God: I am content to do it; yea, thy law is within my heart. I have declared thy righteousness in the great congregation: lo, I will not refrain my lips, O Lord, and that thou knowest. I have not hid thy righteousness within my heart: my talk hath been of thy truth and of thy salvation. I have not kept back thy loving mercy and truth: from the great congregation. Withdraw not thou thy mercy from me, O Lord: let thy loving-kindness and thy truth always preserve me.

For innumerable troubles are come about me; my sins have taken such hold upon me that I am not able to look up: yea, they are more in number than the hairs of my head, and my heart hath failed me. O Lord, let it be thy pleasure to deliver me: make haste, O Lord, to help me. Let them be ashamed and confounded together, that seek after my soul to destroy it: let them be driven backward and put to rebuke, that wish me evil. Let them be desolate, and rewarded with shame: that say unto me, Fie upon thee, fie upon thee. Let all those that seek thee be joyful and glad in thee: and let such as love thy salvation say always, The Lord be praised.

As for me, I am poor and needy: but the Lord careth for me. Thou art my helper and redeemer: make no long tarrying, O my God.

PSALM 40

JAMIE HOWISON

One of the features that makes Psalm 40 rather unique is its inversion of the expected order of things. The psalm has three "movements": a thanksgiving for rescue (vv. 1-5), the theme of sacrifice and of God's will (vv. 6-10), and finally a request for deliverance (vv. 11-17). As Schaefer points out, the usual order of such movements in the Psalms would have us expect the "request for deliverance" to precede any "thanksgiving."[35] I think that in this unexpected inversion we can see the imprint of a mature poet; or more significantly, of a mature believer. It is one thing to go through trials and come out the other side with a song of relief and thanksgiving; it is quite another to be able to stop mid-experience and offer this kind of a reflection as to what is really going on. Let me unpack what I hear in this psalm, to hopefully demonstrate for you what I mean.

---

[35] Konrad Schaefer, OSB, *Psalms; Berit Olam: studies in Hebrew Narrative and Poetry* (Collegeville, Minnesota: A Michael Glazier Book published by The Liturgical Press, 2001), p. 99.

The first five verses speak of having waited in patience for the purely gracious act of rescue at the hand of God:

> I waited patiently for the Lord;
> he inclined to me and heard my cry.
> He drew me up from the desolate pit,
> out of the miry bog,
> and set my feet upon a rock,
> making my steps secure.
> (Psalm 40:1-2)

Notice that while the waiting is characterized as patient, it is not silent, for God "heard my cry." This, I suggest, is the first sign of the writer's spiritual maturity—that there is no apparent contradiction between patience and complaint or lament. The ensuing experience of rescue from the "desolate pit" and "miry bog" is sufficiently powerful to give the singer a "new song" and an expanded sense of the "wondrous deeds" of God:

> He put a new song in my mouth,
> a song of praise to our God.
> Many will see and fear,
> and put their trust in the Lord.
> (Psalm 40:3)

More than this, the experience has been one of such power that it has relativized a whole way of understanding what God requires. God does not require sacrifice and offering, but rather open ears, an open heart, and a mouth open to sing the song far and wide.

> I have not hidden your saving help within my heart,
> I have spoken of your faithfulness and your salvation;
> I have not concealed your steadfast love and your
> faithfulness from the great congregation.
> (Psalm 40:10)

One could reasonably expect Psalm 40 to close right there with verse 10, but instead it goes on to say, in effect, that the ground has once again gone boggy.

> Do not, O Lord, withhold
> your mercy from me;
> let your steadfast love and your faithfulness
> keep me safe forever.
> For evils have encompassed me
> without number;
> my iniquities have overtaken me
> until I cannot see;
> they are more than the hairs of my head,
> and my heart fails me.
> (Psalm 40:11-12)

Verses 11-17 attest to the presence of enemies and evil, and of an experience of being (again or still?) poor and needy. What is more, the verses speak not of being innocently and undeservedly attacked by hostile enemies, but rather of "evils" and, quite explicitly, of "my iniquities." This is a poet who has wrestled, and is wrestling, with being complicit in the evil and disaster of his situation, and who is able to confess the truth with boldness. From the midst of this self-knowledge the psalmist is able to sing of the deep awareness of crisis, rescue, and a reoriented life in God. "I've been there before, and you are steadfast. I will be there again, and you are steadfast." This expression of faith is the maturity of the psalmist's heart and vision.

Steve "gets it" when he takes a chorus praying that God not "withhold your steadfast love and mercy from me," and sandwiches it between a verse that celebrates rescue and one which proclaims far and wide the experience of rescue. Similarly, the Irish rock band U2 "gets it" when, in their song "40," they build two verses around this psalm's themes of thanksgiving and proclamation ("many will see – many will see and hear"[36]). Yet they also contextualize the whole song with a line drawn from the heart of the prophet Isaiah: "How long to sing this song?"[37] Having known rescue and reorientation, faithful singers can balance an expression of trust with a plea for continued love and mercy,

---

[36] U2, "40," *War* (Island Record, 1983)
[37] *Ibid.*

and find no contradiction. In this way, they express the mystery of a fluid, living, and honest faith. "Lord I believe; help thou my unbelief" (Mark 9:24).

STEVE BELL

It's hard to recall now just how insecure I felt in my early adult years. I still have feelings of insecurity to be sure, but they're not as desperate as they once were.

As you've already read, I come from a family with a rich faith heritage. My paternal grandparents were missionaries in China for thirty years in the first half of the last century. My father, born in China, grew to be a marvelous pastor/preacher. As much as I loved my dear father, who is probably the most affirming person I've ever known, I felt the weight of his significance like a low-cloud day. I would simply never measure up. I was a lowly bar musician with chidingly bad habits, and no vision for a better future.

After ten years in the bars, I put my guitar down and started to look for another way to make a living. I was very weary, and I realize now that I was quite broken from a decade-long failed attempt at a career. But then, quite unexpectedly, these songs started to come... these songs you are reading about and listening to. A local pastor heard a cassette tape of some of them and asked me to sing at his church. I said no several times before he wooed me with the promise of financial compensation. I was filled with terror the night I stepped onto that stage, but something happened that I can't adequately explain. A dam broke, and a river began to flow—stories started flowing out of me I had never thought to tell. And as the lyrics and the melodies bathed and cleansed my own soul, and the souls of the few that had gathered for a Sunday evening service, I felt, to borrow a phrase from Eric Liddel, "the pleasure of God."

I cried in the car all the way home. I'm crying now. This song came the next morning.

By the way, I no longer believe in so-called "lowly" bar musicians. I have deep respect and gratitude for every one.

Psalm 40
music and lyric adaptation by Steve Bell

> I patiently waited for you
> A desolate waiting for you
> And you heard my cry oh Lord
> You pulled me from miry bog
> And you set me upon a rock
> And made my steps secure oh Lord
> You put a new song in my heart
> A new song of praise to my God
>
> *Do not thou oh Lord*
> *Withhold your steadfast love*
> *And mercy from me*
> *Mercy from me*
> *Do not thou oh Lord*
> *Withhold your steadfast love*
> *Mercy from me*
>
> I told the great congregation
> The good news of your salvation
> I could not conceal it anymore
> Blessed are those who seek you
> Trusting your love they seek you
> Always saying great is the Lord
> You put a new song in their hearts
> A new song of praise to their God

PSALM 16

PRESERVE me, O God: for in thee have I put my trust. O my soul, thou hast said unto the Lord: Thou art my God, my goods are nothing unto thee. All my delight is upon the saints, that are in the earth: and upon such as excel in virtue. But they that run after another god: shall have great trouble. Their drink-offerings of blood will I not offer: neither make mention of their names within my lips.

The Lord himself is the portion of mine inheritance, and of my cup: thou shalt maintain my lot. The lot is fallen unto me in a fair ground: yea, I have a goodly heritage.

I will thank the Lord for giving me warning: my reins also chasten me in the night-season. I have set God always before me: for he is on my right hand, therefore I shall not fall. Wherefore my heart was glad, and my glory rejoiced: my flesh also shall rest in hope. For why? thou shalt not leave my soul in hell: neither shalt thou suffer thy Holy One to see corruption.

Thou shalt show me the path of life; in thy presence is the fulness of joy: and at thy right hand there is pleasure for evermore.

PSALM 16
I WILL NOT BE SHAKEN

JAMIE HOWISON

Psalm 16 is a celebration of thankfulness for a life experienced as anchored safely in the abiding presence of God. Steve's jazzy, almost ragtime setting catches the psalmist's mood beautifully; so safely is he anchored that it seems to naturally set his feet dancing. Still, it is not an untried or easily won thankfulness. This is not a psalm of easy or safe orientation, but rather one of a deeply grateful yet clear-eyed *reorientation* in the life of God.

There is a fair bit of scholarly debate as to the setting of the psalm. The superscription attributes it to David,[38] but many biblical scholars believe that its language and themes suggest a considerably later date, quite probably following the Israelites' return from the Babylonian Exile. There is a wide consensus among scholars that two main concerns—idolatry and the question of death—burned most brightly in light of the engagement of the exiles with Babylonian culture. In a real sense, though, the question of the psalm's setting is not all that interesting. What should interest us is how those same two concerns burn so brightly in *our* own day,

---

[38] Artur Weiser, *The Psalms* (Philadelphia: The Westminster Press, 1962), p. 172.

and how this psalm has the power to speak with a mature clarity to the worshipper in *these* times.

The opening three verses place both the writer and the "holy ones" safe in the care of a faithful God. Steve's dancing music nails a sense of sheer delight in being so securely anchored in that place.

> Keep me safe, O God you are my refuge
> I say to you Lord – you are my God
> Apart from you I have no good thing going
> As for the saints living in the land
> Those at peace at the Lord's right hand
> I delight in those who are your own.

Yet just as the delight builds, the psalmist introduces a bit of a warning:

> Those who choose another god multiply their sorrows;
> their drink offerings of blood I will not pour out
> or take their names upon my lips.
> (Psalm 16:4)

It is interesting that the original Hebrew text does not actually use the phrase "another god," but rather just the word "others." This psalmist will not even dignify the objects of "other" religious practices as being gods; they are just "others." Offer blood and swear by their names and it will get you only the "nothing" another non-god can give. Worse than nothing, really, because in relying on such illusions you only "multiply sorrows."

We still tend to think of distinct, actual religious idols when we hear the word idolatry, yet in this age we are wise to think instead of all the "others" in which we invest. As Episcopal priest and author Robert Farrar Capon was fond of pointing out, humans are a hopelessly religious bunch.[39] We are always looking to serve *something* in hopes that, through our right practice, we will find happiness and fulfillment. The modern gods include money, sex,

---

[39] Robert Farrar Capon has argued this case in any number of his books, but probably most thoroughly in *Health, Money & Love... and why we don't enjoy them*. (Grand Rapids: William B. Eerdmans Publishing Company, 1990).

fitness, and health, which are propitiated in the temples of bank, bedroom, gym, and medical office. We serve these gods like mad, by working investment portfolios, studying sexual technique, pumping iron, or researching all of the latest internet health links; and they are all blind alleys. No bank account is ever full enough, no sexual pleasure ever intense enough, no stomach ever toned enough... and no one can stave off death forever. They are the "nothing;" but when we invest our lives in them they become all consuming "everythings." Such idolatries consume our entire beings, and then leave us disappointed.

For the psalmist, "The Lord is my chosen portion," and not (not, not!) my six-pack abs, my sex life, or my bank balance.

> Even at night
> Sleep cannot hide
> My Lord, forever at my side

"This is what I see and hear and attend to," sings this ancient poet. Not an idol or "another," but the Lord who is "always before me."

The psalmist has found a peace with this way of being in the world, telling the reader that all things considered, even matters of property and financial security are just fine, thank you very much.

> The boundary lines have fallen for me in pleasant
> places; I have a goodly heritage.
> (Psalm 16:6)

The psalmist has a decent piece of land and a respectable nest-egg to leave to the children. Is this happiness on account of having done well financially? Or is the writer happy with whatever (modest?) security has come, because there has first been a foundational security of being in the presence of God? Considering how the psalmist now turns and focuses attention on questions of death and life suggests to me that the latter is at work. Because this psalmist is secure in relation to God, contentment has come, and even death poses no great threat.

> Therefore my heart is glad, and my soul rejoices;

my body also rests secure.
For you do not give me up to She'ol,
or let your faithful one see the Pit.
You show me the path of life.
In your presence there is fullness of joy;
in your right hand are pleasures forevermore.
(Psalm 16:9-11)

It is significant to recall that for the Hebrew imagination, human life was not seen in terms of a spirit or soul encased in a body; nor was eternal life thought to be the freeing of an immortal soul from a limiting physical body. Human life was lived in terms of a unified body/soul, and death marked the end of that life. As a theology of eternal life develops through the Hebrew scriptures (coming to fruition in the New Testament, and particularly in the writings of the apostle Paul), it is always a proclamation of *resurrection*, not of an eternal soul.[40] When the psalmist contemplates death, he is dealing with his whole, human body/soul self. And quite frankly, what we see is a writer untroubled by the prospect of that death, for this anchoring trust in God has given him a deep and foundational security. In considering these verses, Artur Weiser suggests that the psalmist has reached an extraordinary place in his life:

> By reaching a deeper religious insight into the meaning of life, the worshipper, in fact, considers the problem of death as no longer the most crucial question. To the life-giving power of God in which the poet is privileged to share, death and the underworld are no insurmountable obstacles which could shatter that living communion with God.[41]

As Paul writes,

For I am convinced that neither *death*, nor life, nor

---

[40] One of the best treatments of this topic is found in a little book by the German evangelical scholar Oscar Cullmann, entitled *Immortality of the Soul or Resurrection of the Dead?* (London: The Epworth Press, 1958).
[41] Weiser, p. 178.

angels, nor rulers, nor things present, nor things to come, nor powers, nor height, nor depth, nor anything else in all creation, will be able to separate us from the love of God in Christ Jesus our Lord.
(Romans 8:38-39, italics added)

Few of us, of course, find ourselves feeling quite so secure all of the time. The prospect of death—of ourselves or of those we love—continues to unsettle or frighten or even appall us. All the more reason to sing this psalm.

STEVE BELL

Who can say why one day you read a passage of scripture and are unmoved, and the next day, the same passage sets a fire in your belly? The Bible from my youth is full of single and double underlined sections, with exclamations and scribbled notes that make no sense to me now; whereas I'm dumbfounded by the passages I left untouched. There came a day when Psalm 16 surprisingly leapt off the page and stirred me enough to know I wanted to write it as a song. No matter how hard I tried however, nothing would come. I was listening to a lot of Michael Card and John Michael Talbot in those days, and was trying unsuccessfully to emulate their contemplative, folk music writing style with this psalm.

Then one night, I saw Leo Kottke in concert. I was a big fan of his guitar playing but had no idea how he managed the astonishing rhythm and percussion of his style until I saw him perform live. Suddenly, during the concert, I understood (in part) what he was doing. When I got home that night I worked for several hours trying to get a handle on his technique. Psalm 16 happened to be on a piece of paper on the table in front of me. As I was getting the hang of the technique, a melody started to form and I recognized its compatibility with the psalm lyric. The song that came was entirely different in mood and style from what I was initially trying to write—but it remains one of my favourite songs of all I've written.

I Will Not Be Shaken
music and lyric adaptation by Steve Bell

Keep me safe, O God you are my refuge
I say to you Lord, you are my God
Apart from you I have no good thing going
As for the saints living in the land
Those at peace at the Lord's right hand
I delight in those who are your own

Lord you've given me my cup and portion
Again I say you've made my lot secure
The boundary lines they fall in pleasant places
Surely I have a rightful place
Filled with joy at the throne of grace
There I'll praise your name forever more

Even at night
Sleep will not hide
My Lord forever at my side
I will not be shaken
I will not be shaken
No, no I will not be shaken
With you by my side

Therefore now my heart and tongue rejoices
Therefore now my body rests secure
I am filled with joy within your presence
You'll not leave me in the grave
Or let your holy ones decay
You have given me the way of life

PSALM 32

BLESSED is he whose unrighteousness is forgiven: and whose sin is covered. Blessed is the man unto whom the Lord imputeth no sin: and in whose spirit there is no guile.

For while I held my tongue: my bones consumed away through my daily complaining. For thy hand is heavy upon me day and night: and my moisture is like the drought in summer. I will acknowledge my sin unto thee: and mine unrighteousness have I not hid. I said, I will confess my sins unto the Lord: and so thou forgavest the wickedness of my sin.

For this shall every one that is godly make his prayer unto thee, in a time when thou mayest be found: but in the great water-floods they shall not come nigh him. Thou art a place to hide me in, thou shalt preserve me from trouble: thou shalt compass me about with songs of deliverance.

I will inform thee, and teach thee in the way wherein thou shalt go: and I will guide thee with mine eye. Be ye not like to horse and mule, which have no understanding: whose mouths must be held with bit and bridle, lest they fall upon thee. Great plagues remain for the ungodly: but whoso putteth his trust in the Lord, mercy embraceth him on every side.

Be glad, O ye righteous, and rejoice in the Lord: and be joyful, all ye that are true of heart.

PSALM 32

JAMIE HOWISON

One of the great lies that gets attached to matters of faith and religion is that sinners have all the fun. Bolstered by shallow media stereotypes, it is nevertheless a view held (consciously or otherwise) and perpetuated by many Christians. To be a Christian, the argument goes, is to *behave* and so to avoid eternal punishment. "Store up your treasures in heaven" is corrupted to become something more like "deny the gratification of those deliciously wicked desires, and in the end you'll do better than the sinners."

Thirty years ago, when I was a seminary student in Toronto, one of my professors trotted our "Christian Apologetics" class off to attend a debate on the existence of God. The man arguing for the reasonableness of a belief in God was a visiting professor of philosophy from an American evangelical college. I have long since forgotten both his name and the name of his college, but I will never forget what he said about the "moral coherence" of a belief in God. It is self-evident, he said, that on this side of the grave justice is only partial: children die, the wicked prosper, crimes go unpunished, righteous people suffer, and so on. Therefore, he concluded, it is reasonable to believe in an order beyond this one, in which true justice will be done. Anyone familiar with the classic arguments and "proofs" for God's existence will know this is not a new or original position. It was, however, his illustrative anecdote that betrayed his deeper position. "I was walking down Yonge Street today," he said, "and saw the strip bars and hookers and porn shops. If there is no higher judgment, what reason is there for me to not take part in all of those things?"

The humanist philosopher who was debating against the need for a belief in God paused, and then quietly said, "Because not taking part in those things is the right thing to do." Although he might be surprised to hear this suggestion, that agnostic philosopher was closer in spirit to Psalm 32 than his Christian opponent. At first glance, "the right thing to do" might seem naïve and simplistic; but this answer actually draws upon the Aristotelian idea of "virtue," and has strong connections to the biblical assumption that the "right thing" (or the thing for which God has created us) is the thing that gives life and light and freedom. As Steve's song explains,

> How blessed are those
> whose sins are fully forgiven.
> How blessed are those
> to whom Yahweh harbors no ill.

In his important commentary on the Psalms, Artur Weiser observes that, "The poet wrote the two 'beatitudes' with which the psalm opens with his heart's blood."[42] This is a poet who knows— who really and truly *knows*—that sin is not deliciously wicked. It is agonizingly disintegrating and distorting. Living with a fragmented self out of harmony with God's intention, the psalmist experiences wasting, heaviness, and heat. This is not the license and glamorous debauch that some people imagine drives the New Orleans Mardi Gras or Rio's Carnival. No, this is the perspective of someone who has experienced life like a vicious morning-after hangover that never lets up.

---

[42] Artur Weiser, *The Psalms* (Philadelphia: The Westminster Press, 1962), p. 283.

So long as the psalmist attempts to keep silent and to manage his own brokenness, the weight remains. It is in speaking the truth— "I acknowledge my sin to you"—that reintegration begins—"you forgave the guilt of my sin." No longer a "heavy hand," God becomes a hiding place, presence, and deliverance. Truth be told, our evangelical philosopher from the preceding debate would not be punished for visiting the hookers on Yonge Street. The time spent with the prostitute and the ensuing disintegration would have been its own distorting and disorienting punishment.[43] As theologian and ethicist Stanley Hauerwas puts it, "the Christian understanding of punishment must begin with the recognition that we are not punished for our sins, but sin is our punishment."[44]

Again from Weiser, Psalm 32 is "one of the Psalter's most powerful testimonies to the struggles and qualms of conscience in which a man is involved who cannot run away from his God."[45] Where can I flee from your presence?" (Psalm 139:7b). No place of refuge is available, this psalm rhetorically replies. The choices are to remain silent and distorted, or to speak truthfully and find not a refuge *from* God but a hiding place *in* God.

---

[43] I know of no better illustration of this point than John Updike's short story "Transaction." In the story, a married businessman on an out-of-town trip decides to engage the services of a prostitute. There is a brief exploration of the man's thought process, but it all leads to the story's end, as the man realizes that now he must live with the knowledge and experience of having made sexual intimacy into a transaction. While the narrative is quite sexually explicit, it is utterly without erotic or sensual appeal. It is sadly ironic, then, that "Transaction" was first published in *Oui*, a now defunct "men's magazine." John Updike, "Transaction," *Problems and other stories* (New York: Fawcett Crest, 1981), pp. 102-131.

[44] Stanley Hauerwas, "Punishing Christians," *Performing the Faith* (Grand Rapids, Michigan: Brazos Press, 2004), p. 198.

[45] Weiser, p. 282.

STEVE BELL

I wrote this song for my father. When I first started to play music in the bars, I initially hid this knowledge from my dad for several months. I didn't do this because I thought my dad would be angry—Dad was not an angry sort, and he had always shown generous support for everything I put my hand to. But somehow I couldn't imagine that he could be proud of me as a bar musician and I loathed the thought of disappointing him. I eventually had to come clean though, and when I did, instead of showing disappointment or disapproval, my father blessed me. Literally! He leaned over, put his hands on my shoulders, lifted his eyes to heaven, and he blessed me. I was more than a little shocked. Had I known this was an option, I would have come clean much earlier.

The next night he showed up at the bar where I was performing and spent the night with my buddies and me. This was not something one would expect from a Baptist minister in the late 1970s. But afterward, when I stopped to think about it, Dad's response was entirely in character for the man I had always known. My own sense of shame simply robbed me of my ability to judge him correctly.

Dad later said, "we confuse reward with blessing. A reward is given at the end of a race for a job well done. Blessing properly comes at the beginning of a race so that a job can be well done."

I wrote this song years later when I read Psalm 32 and recognized in it some of my own story.

Psalm 32
music and lyric adaptation by Steve Bell

> How blessed are those
> Whose sins are fully forgiven
> How blessed are those
> To whom Yahweh harbours no ill
> To whom his spirit is known

I said not a word
And my bones they wasted away
From groaning all day and night
Your hand lay heavy upon me
My heart grew thirsty so I...

Made myself known to you
I did not hide
My shameful soul
My darkest side
And you loved me
And held me
And you forgave my sin

That is why each
One of your faithful ones prays to you
In times of distress
Though dark rivers overflow
You'll never loosen your hold
For I know it's true
You are a refuge always for me
You guard me with hope
With songs of deliverance
Surrounding me so I...

Made myself known to you
I did not hide
My shameful soul
My darkest side
And you loved me
And held me
And you forgave my sin

PSALM 25

UNTO thee, O Lord, will I lift up my soul; my God, I have put
my trust in thee: O let me not be confounded, neither let mine
enemies triumph over me. For all they that hope in thee shall not
be ashamed: but such as transgress without a cause shall be put to
confusion.

Show me thy ways, O Lord: and teach me thy paths. Lead me forth
in thy truth, and learn me: for thou art the God of my salvation; in
thee hath been my hope all the day long. Call to remembrance, O
Lord, thy tender mercies: and thy loving-kindnesses, which have
been ever of old. O remember not the sins and offences of my youth:
but according to thy mercy think thou upon me,
O Lord, for thy goodness.

Gracious and righteous is the Lord: therefore will he teach sinners
in the way. Them that are meek shall he guide in judgement: and
such as are gentle, them shall he learn his way. All the paths of the
Lord are mercy and truth: unto such as keep his covenant and his
testimonies. For thy Name's sake, O Lord: be merciful unto my sin,
for it is great. What man is he that feareth the Lord: him shall he
teach in the way that he shall choose. His soul shall dwell at ease:
and his seed shall inherit the land. The secret of the Lord is among
them that fear him: and he will show them his covenant. Mine eyes
are ever looking unto the Lord: for he shall pluck my feet out of the
net.

Turn thee unto me, and have mercy upon me: for I am desolate and
in misery. The sorrows of my heart are enlarged: O bring thou me
out of my troubles. Look upon my adversity and misery: and forgive
me all my sin. Consider mine enemies, how many they are: and
they bear a tyrannous hate against me. O keep my soul, and deliver
me: let me not be confounded, for I have put my trust in thee. Let
perfectness and righteous dealing wait upon me: for my hope hath
been in thee.

Deliver Israel, O God: out of all his troubles.

CHAPTER 9

PSALM 25
REMEMBER ME

JAMIE HOWISON

Memory and the act of remembering play a vital role in the story of Israel. Glancing through my battered copy of *Cruden's Concordance* (first published in 1737, and so working with the King James Version), I notice that while "memory" appears a scant five times in the Old Testament, there are well over a hundred citations of the word "remember." Starting with God *remembering* Noah in the midst of the flood (Gen 8:1), the stage is set for the long dance of memory in scripture. God *remembers* Abraham (Gen 19:29) and Rachel (Gen 30:22). As Exodus opens, we are told how after Joseph died, a new Pharaoh arose in Egypt, "who did not know Joseph"—who had no memory of the hospitality extended by his forebears to these Hebrews—and so begins the slavery and oppression of the people. During the wilderness wanderings of those freed slaves, they are instructed to "*remember* and do all my commandments, and you shall be holy to your God" (Numbers 15:40).

Yet they remember not. At various points in their forty-year desert time, these people evidence an extraordinary propensity to forget yesterday's grace. In the Promised Land, first as a tribal league administered by the judges, and later as a nation with a king, they keep lapsing into a deep forgetfulness as to who—and *whose*—they are. Under the weight of this collective amnesia, Israel collapses. First the northern kingdom is shattered in 722 BCE, and then in 586 BCE the southern kingdom falls to the Babylonians. The kingdoms collapse precisely because God, forgotten and jealous, ceases to buttress such a forgetful people.

At this point in their history a terrible realization begins to set in, most poignantly and horrifically voiced in Lamentations:

> Jerusalem remembers in the days of her
> affliction and wanderings,
> all the precious things that were hers in days of old.
> When her people fell into the hand of the foe,
> and there was no one to help her,
> the foe looked on mocking her downfall.
> (Lamentations 1:7)

> Remember, O Lord, what has befallen us;
> look, and see our disgrace!
> (Lamentations 5:1)

> Why have you forgotten us completely?
> Why have you forsaken us these many days?
> Restore us to yourself, O Lord,
> that we may be restored;
> renew our days as of old –
> unless you have utterly rejected us,
> and are angry with us beyond measure.
> (Lamentations 5:20-22)

The horror is that after so many generations of Israel *not* remembering to whom they belong, God seems now to have voluntarily forgotten them.

The psalmist picks up this issue of remembrance in verse 7 of Psalm 25:

> Do not remember the sins of my youth or my
> transgressions; according to your steadfast love
> remember me, for your goodness sake, O Lord!
> (Psalm 25:7)

It is this verse, of course, which gives focus to Steve's song, "Remember Me." The repeated line, "in your love remember me" should haunt us, as we so often and so easily forget. The "sins of my youth" are almost weightless compared to the continued sin of today. Will I be remembered, even now, as I continue to do and think and say the things I *know* to be borne of brokenness?

The prophet Isaiah dares an answer, and one that almost directly parallels the horror of Lamentations.

> Can a woman forget her nursing child,
> or show no compassion for the child of her womb?
> Even these may forget,
> yet I will not forget you.
> See, I have inscribed you on the palms of my hands;
> your walls are continually before me.
> (Isaiah 49:15-16)

"I will not forget you." All evidence to the contrary—and there was a great deal of evidence in the burning streets of a desolated Jerusalem, including mothers *eating* their own children (Lamentations 5:10)—God has not forgotten.

Yet along with Steve we must reply, "in your *love* remember me." I don't want to be remembered in a cool or dispassionate way. I don't want a blindfolded Lady Justice weighing my sins on her scales. I'll utterly fail. But rather, in your *love* remember me.

It is on the cross that God proclaims a deep and profound distaste for blindfolds. There is no blind justice on Golgotha, and there is no scorecard at the gates to the New Jerusalem. If Lamentations speaks from a place of fear that God has voluntarily forgotten and forsaken the people of Israel, the cross speaks a powerful counter-word about God having effectively chosen to take an amnesia pill regarding our sin. On the cross, the dream of Psalm 25 has gone one better: not only are the sins of our youth forgotten, but everything that threatens to separate us from the love of God—either in the past, present, or future—is tossed on the garbage heap. The only thing remaining is us, the unworthy yet inexplicably beloved "apple of God's eye" (Psalm 17:8). That is worth remembering the next time you catch yourself thinking about doing something foolish.

STEVE BELL

My dad used to say that guilt is a good thing—like the nerve endings in your fingers that warn you when you've placed your hand on something hot. When you lose that sensitivity, it's called leprosy, which was a disease Jesus was particularly keen to heal, restoring to the afflicted person the life-saving gift of pain.

Shame however, is entirely different. Dad would say whereas guilt is feeling bad for something you've done, shame is feeling bad for who you are. One is life saving, and the other life destroying. The distinction is vital.

I can no longer remember the details that precipitated the writing of this song. But, clearly I was coming to terms with my past, making peace with God and with myself, and beginning to trust that I was an irrevocable part of something eternally good. For as shame alienates and dis-members, love integrates and re-members.

Remember Me
music and lyric adaptation by Steve Bell

> To you alone do I lift up my soul
> You are the only recourse that I know
> When shame denies me a place in your fold
> In your love remember me

Show me a road with respect to the truth
Hold not against me the sins of my youth
There's no one to turn to if you don't come through
In your love remember me

In your love remember me
In your love remember me
All because of your goodness Lord
In your love remember me

Yahweh confides in the ones who have faith
And shares from the secrets of old so they say
Dare I presume he would treat me the same
In your love remember me

Show me your favour Yahweh
Go ahead and correct me for the sake of your name
It is your reputation that makes me outrageously brave
Hold out your mercy to me
Go ahead and correct me for the sake of your name
It's not much of a thread
by my hoping is keeping me sane
Again and again...

PSALM 84

O HOW amiable are thy dwellings: thou Lord of hosts! My soul hath a desire and longing to enter into the courts of the Lord: my heart and my flesh rejoice in the living God.

Yea, the sparrow hath found her an house, and the swallow a nest where she may lay her young: even thy altars, O Lord of hosts, my King and my God.

Blessed are they that dwell in thy house: they will be always praising thee. Blessed is the man whose strength is in thee: in whose heart are thy ways. Who going through the vale of misery use it for a well: and the pools are filled with water. They will go from strength to strength: and unto the God of gods appeareth every one of them in Sion.

O Lord God of hosts, hear my prayer: hearken, O God of Jacob. Behold, O God our defender: and look upon the face of thine Anointed.

For one day in thy courts: is better than a thousand. I had rather be a door-keeper in the house of my God: than to dwell in the tents of ungodliness. For the Lord God is a light and defence: the Lord will give grace and worship, and no good thing shall he withhold from them that live a godly life. O Lord God of hosts: blessed is the man that putteth his trust in thee.

CHAPTER 10

PSALM 84
GOD OUR PROTECTOR

JAMIE HOWISON

While the original Psalm 84 is a pilgrim song celebrating the Jerusalem temple as the high point—and actual physical location—for spiritual fulfillment, in Steve's hands the closing verses become a prayer for an engagement with a God *not* tied to place. For the Christian, this shift is not only a valid reframing of these verses, but is also a necessary and faithful turn. Watch.

In ancient Israel, the temple was "the house of God" (Ps. 84:10), or at least as close to a "house" as this unfettered God was likely to have. Whether Solomon's temple, the temple of Zerubbabel (the "second temple," constructed after the Babylonian exile), or Herod's temple (the one which Jesus visited), this was the place in society and culture that seemed to focus and express the holiness and presence of God. More than just a place of ritual observance, the temple embodied the hopes and dreams of this people and their faith. While always part of the visual horizon for the citizens of Jerusalem, for other Israelites it was the focus of pilgrimage. Perhaps for moderns, the closest parallel we can see is the Islamic *haj*, the great pilgrimage to the city of Mecca. Life for the devout

84

Muslim is said to be forever changed in light of the *haj*. Life for the Israelite was similarly transformed by pilgrimage to the temple, though the experience might be repeated again and again, even yearly. The pilgrim might have to travel through desolate wilderness— "the valley of Baca" (Ps. 84:6)—to get to the temple, yet in the process might find the wilderness figuratively changed into a place of lushness.

> Happy are those whose strength is in you,
> in whose heart are the highways to Zion.
> As they go through the valley of Baca
> they make it a place of springs;
> the early rain also covers it with pools
> (Psalm 84:5-6)

The temple was so greatly esteemed that people were said to envy even the birds that nested in its precincts (Ps. 84:3), to say nothing of the servants who actually lived there.

> Even the sparrow finds a home,
> and the swallow a nest for herself,
> where she may lay her young
> at your altars, O Lord of hosts,
> my King and my God.
> Happy are those who live in your house,
> ever singing your praise.
> (Psalm 84:3-4)

A single day in the temple is celebrated as superior to a thousand days lived anywhere else. Better to be a doorman—or even a beggar for that matter[46]—at the doorway to the house of God than to live in decadent comfort elsewhere. This is serious stuff!

Part of what should strike us as remarkable is the degree to which

---

[46] Wieser sees the force of this phrase as implying the role of a beggar, standing and waiting for alms at the temple threshold: "he would rather stand like a beggar at the threshold of the house of God in burning sunshine than dwell in the cool shadow of the tents with the godless Gentiles." Artur Weiser *The Psalms* p. 569.

the pilgrim feels at home and rooted in a place that is not, strictly speaking, his or her hometown. This temple, this city, this physical *place*, draws and roots the pilgrim Jew in an almost startling way.

So what happens when the temple is no more? For Judaism, it has meant a deep immersion in biblical text, complemented by a set of disciplines and observances carried out in home and community. For Christians, though, there is the proclamation of a new temple: "He spoke of the temple of his body" (John 2:21). The temple is Christ Jesus, and to dwell in the temple is to dwell in him; in his Body that is his church, and in his Spirit. However much we might love our church buildings and sacred spaces, physical location is entirely secondary. Biblically, in fact, buildings have always been secondary, for the deep tradition of ancient Israel knew that even the grandest space could never contain this God.

Steve's song is a prayer that we might become as aware of the presence and power of God as those pilgrims were attuned to the Jerusalem temple. God is proclaimed as protector—"For the Lord God is a sun and shield" (Ps. 84:11)—and the prayer is offered that this protector would be mindful of us and a strength to us. "For if we could be with you," Steve sings, yet where else could we be but in the presence of the God in whom all things have their being?

> If we could be with you
> One day in time
> It is better than a thousand without you.

As the temple once focused the awareness of our forebears, may all things now deepen the awareness of life lived in your presence, O Lord. That is the force of this song we sing. That is the force of our faith.

STEVE BELL

I often led worship at my church in the 1980s and '90s. One Sunday morning, I felt like I didn't have an adequate opening song, and so I turned to the Catholic missalette, a resource I often used for inspiration when planning services. The entrance antiphon for the day was taken from Psalm 84, and it struck me as a wonderful opening prayer to sing together. Given I was only trying to write something to serve the congregation that morning, I allowed myself a simplicity I may not have, had I thought I was writing for concerts and recording.

God Our Protector
music and lyric adaptation by Steve Bell

> God our protector
> Keep us in mind
> Always give strength to your people
> For if we could be with you
> One day in time
> It is better than a thousand without you

PSALM 113

PRAISE the Lord, ye servants: O praise the Name of the Lord. Blessed be the Name of the Lord: from this time forth for evermore. The Lord's Name is praised: from the rising up of the sun unto the going down of the same.

The Lord is high above all heathen: and his glory above the heavens. Who is like unto the Lord our God, that hath his dwelling so high: and yet humbleth himself to behold the things that are in heaven and earth? He taketh up the simple out of the dust: and lifteth the poor out of the mire; That he may set him with the princes: even with the princes of his people. He maketh the barren woman to keep house: and to be a joyful mother of children.

CHAPTER 11

PSALM 113
HIGH ABOVE THE FRAY

JAMIE HOWISON

"Praise and worship" has become a kind of catch-phrase for a particular sort of worship music. When someone speaks of "praise and worship" (sometimes maddeningly shortened in print to "P & W"), they are usually referring to highly singable, almost anthemic songs of celebration and affirmation. Certainly what is being affirmed is God—God's goodness, God's love, God's mercy—yet the overall impact is often to affirm the security of the worshipper in relation to God. Which is not an entirely bad thing, so far as it goes; but as a *primary* vocabulary it can wear a bit thin. What happens when life deals a different hand to the worshipper? What if on *this* night, praise and worship is a language without sufficient depth and resonance to speak to what is really going on in my life and in the life of this Christian community?

Psalm 113 is a hymn of praise, yet it is not "thin" in the way of those "P & W" songs, for even as it praises the name of the Lord, it manages to name two social realities in need of God's care:

He raises the poor from the dust,

89

and lifts the needy from the ash heap.
(Psalm 113:7)

He gives the barren woman a home,
making her the joyous mother of children.
(Psalm 113:9)

The Lord *does* this, or is *doing* this, or will *do* this; these are not forgotten people, and they are not judged for their poverty or barrenness. This psalm is remarkably free of any moralizing that tries to assign blame to the poor or the childless for their current states. Instead, these people are recognized as people in need, and their liberation is proclaimed as a matter of God's work... and by extension, the work of God's people.

Steve's setting for his song takes an interesting interpretive turn, and presses home this insight.

Let every weary doubter be assured
It is he
High above the fray

The original psalm includes no direct reference to a "weary doubter," yet the psalmist's assumption is that many who sing the psalm are likely to be coming with weariness and doubt. Whatever our own particular poverty or barrenness, if we are at all honest about ourselves, we will know that we are among the "needy." What is it this week? Overworked, or over-worried, or overwhelmed? As a parent or partner or pastor or person?

The Lord is high above all nations,
and his glory above the heavens.
(Psalm 113:4)

In its original context, this proclamation had much to do with Israel's national consciousness as God's people amongst the nations. Steve's shift from "the nations" to "the fray" works nicely in a Christian context, in which we occasionally manage to grasp that our citizenship is in the kingdom of heaven; that "the nations" have been given relative status in the eyes of God; and that "the nations" are in fact inevitably caught up in "the fray." But do we believe this? Ever since the Roman emperor Constantine converted to Christianity, we have been tempted to claim *this* empire or *that* nation as being uniquely God's project—"one nation under God," and so on. I am a Canadian of Scottish ancestry, and can be darn proud of it. However, when I take the scripture in its disarming fullness, I have to grapple with the truth of my citizenship in the kingdom of God and my status as a Gentile grafted on to the root that is Israel. "The world is circumcised in the circumcision of Jesus," commented Robert Farrar Capon, "and we are made Jews."[47] All other identity—national, ethnic, racial—is just a part of the fray.

And so yes, we praise. We say, "blessed be the name of the Lord," and we dare to imagine the poor sitting with princes:

> Who is like the Lord our God,
> who is seated on high,
> who looks far down
> upon the heavens and the earth?
> He raises the poor from the dust,
> and lifts the needy from the ash heap,
> to make them sit with princes,
> with the princes of his people.
> (Psalm 113:7-8)

We knowing there is but one kingdom in which this is really possible. And as we praise the God of that kingdom, we dare to imagine there is also a place for us.

---

[47] Robert Farrar Capon, unpublished interview, Shelter Island, NY, January 13, 2004.

STEVE BELL

I've never been very good at prayer, as my mind is far too easily distracted by "shiny things." But over the years, certain psalms have become my prayers as they inspired reflection and melody. Long ago I realized that the very process of songwriting (especially with the Psalms) is how I've been uniquely blessed to focus and to pray.

This song came at a time when Nanci and I went through a string of tragedies over a period of several weeks—a deluge of unrelated crises that seemed like they'd never stop. At a time when you'd think a reminder of how God was "near and dear" would be important, my consolation came from a psalm that reminded me that God was "high above the fray." Somehow, I found that to be *very* comforting.

High Above the Fray
music and lyric adaptation by Steve Bell

> From the rising of the sun
> To the setting of the same
> Who is like the one who is our maker
> Every citizen belongs
> To a nation and a name
> But high above these things is their keeper
>
> *Blessed be the name of the Lord*
> *My heart pounds out this praise*
> *Let every weary doubter be assured*
> *It is he! High above the fray*
>
> And he picks up from the dust
> Every lost and lonely wretch
> Inviting them to come to the table
> And he honours them among
> The brightest and the best
> Who could have guessed, no one is able

PSALM 92

IT IS a good thing to give thanks unto the Lord: and to sing praises unto thy Name, O most Highest; To tell of thy loving-kindness early in the morning: and of thy truth in the night-season; Upon an instrument of ten strings, and upon the lute: upon a loud instrument, and upon the harp. For thou, Lord, hast made me glad through thy works: and I will rejoice in giving praise for the operations of thy hands. O Lord, how glorious are thy works: thy thoughts are very deep. An unwise man doth not well consider this: and a fool doth not understand it. When the ungodly are green as the grass, and when all the workers of wickedness do flourish: then shall they be destroyed for ever; but thou, Lord, art the most Highest for evermore. For lo, thine enemies, O Lord, lo, thine enemies shall perish: and all the workers of wickedness shall be destroyed.

But mine horn shall be exalted like the horn of an unicorn: for I am anointed with fresh oil. Mine eye also shall see his lust of mine enemies: and mine ear shall hear his desire of the wicked that arise up against me.

The righteous shall flourish like a palm-tree: and shall spread abroad like a cedar in Libanus. Such as are planted in the house of the Lord: shall flourish in the courts of the house of our God. They also shall bring forth more fruit in their age: and shall be fat and well-liking. That they may show how true the Lord my strength is: and that there is no unrighteousness in him.

PSALM 92
FRESH AND GREEN

JAMIE HOWISON

Psalm 92 stands in celebration of what I would call a "long haul" kind of faith. Right from the opening verses, it is all about giving thanks for the steadfastness of God's love, and doing so with music and with steady, rhythmic, even liturgical prayer. In all likelihood, the phrases "in the morning" and "by night" point to a pattern of regular, ordered daily prayer: the sort of praying that is nurtured through sustained practice, such that morning and evening are each incomplete without moving to God in prayer. This is the sort of prayer life, in fact, most of us attempt to cultivate again and again over the course of many years, until one day (provided that we keep chipping away at the discipline...) it is finally just *there*. This practice is a big part of the "long haul" work-a-day kind of faith that is ours as Christians.

It isn't very sexy or flashy, this long haul stuff. Other methods and styles and ways of being give the illusion of flourishing prosperity— "the wicked sprout like grass and all evildoers flourish" (vs. 7)—but in the end, these all collapse on themselves. In contrast, the long haul kind of faithfulness yields something with roots deep enough to sustain real growth.

> The righteous flourish like the palm tree,
> and grow like a cedar in Lebanon.
> (Psalm 92:12)

But that kind of growth is long and slow, and virtually impossible to measure day by day. That kind of growth is about a patience that refuses the allure of the quick fix. That kind of growth is not always easy. In fact, tucked right into the text is a touch of what could easily become arrogance.

> The dullard cannot know,
> the stupid cannot understand this:
> though the wicked sprout like grass
> and all evil doers flourish,
> they are doomed to destruction forever.
> (Psalm 92:6-7)

> But you have exalted *my* horn like that of the wild ox;
> you have poured over *me* fresh oil.
> (Psalm 92:10, italics added)

"Don't mind me... I'm just quietly growing stronger here in my righteousness. Just wait and watch me flourish, while the evildoers get theirs..." If Psalm 92 doesn't go quite that far, you can see how someone might begin to slip into such a mindset. That sort of attitude isn't steadfastness of belief or true righteousness of life, but rather something closer to self-righteousness. Pray with the psalmist, but beware the trap.

The richest image—and the one that Steve picks up on for his song—is saved until the second last verse:

> In old age they still produce fruit;
> they are always green and full of sap.
> (Psalm 92:14)

Or, more poetically, and certainly more aesthetically appealing to the elders of our church communities,

Fresh and green we will remain
Bearing fruit to a ripe old age.

Here we are called away from the self-righteousness which inevitably yields something less "fresh and green" and more grey and brittle. The long haul kind of faith cultivates a people who are at once elders *and* children of God: aged and seasoned and disciplined, yet playful and productive and able to bend and move whenever the winds of the Holy Spirit blow. It is a great and paradoxical image. If you think about it, and reflect on your own encounters with the living saints in your church circles, you'll realize it is an image that also happens to be true.

STEVE BELL

I wrote this song for my mom on the occasion of her becoming a senior citizen. Although my mom has experienced many dark days and years on account of a recurring anxiety disorder, she has also had many bright days and years of wellness and good health. I wrote this in the midst of happy years.

Fresh and Green
music and lyric adaptation by Steve Bell

> *Fresh and green we will remain*
> *Bearing fruit to a ripe old age*
> *Happy to tell about your name*
> *A blessed endeavour*
> *The righteous flourish like the palm*
> *And grow like cedars of Lebanon*
> *Planted in the courts of God*
> *Forever and ever*

> The senseless person doesn't know
> The wonders of your glory
> And yet their hoppers overflow
> But they don't understand

That folly springs up like the grass
And spreads throughout these vast lands
But harvesting will come to pass
When everything is shown
Everything will be exposed

Fresh and green we will remain...

It is so good to sing of you
At the first sight of the morning
And at night your faithfulness review
Before I close my eyes
And sometimes in the dimming light
I stumble on your glory
That overwhelming sudden fright
But not the daunting kind
It's so hard to describe

Fresh and green we will remain...

PSALM 3

LORD, how are they increased that trouble me: many are they that rise against me. Many one there be that say of my soul: There is no help for him in his God. But thou, O Lord, art my defender: thou art my worship, and the lifter up of my head. I did call upon the Lord with my voice: and he heard me out of his holy hill. I laid me down and slept, and rose up again: for the Lord sustained me. I will not be afraid for ten thousands of the people: that have set themselves against me round about.

Up, Lord, and help me, O my God: for thou smitest all mine enemies upon the cheekbone; thou hast broken the teeth of the ungodly. Salvation belongeth unto the Lord: and thy blessing is upon thy people.

PSALM 3
JESUS MY GLORY

JAMIE HOWISON

According to the superscription, Psalm 3 is set in the time when David's son Absalom had mounted a rebellion (the consummate "inside job," when you consider that this was son against father), which forced the great king to flee Jerusalem to try to salvage what looked like an increasingly lost cause. Whatever the later liturgical setting might have been, this story of deep disorientation must have loomed large in the imagination of anyone who later sang it as a form of lament and complaint. Konrad Schaefer observes that Psalm 3 conveys "a liturgical motif which may have been spoken by the priest or royal presider, as the individual complaint articulates a typical crisis of the people."[48] Whatever the "typical crisis" might have been, David and his rebel son would have figured in the background as *the* story of betrayal.

The sense of disorientation here is enormous, with the "many

---

[48] Konrad Schaefer OSB, *Psalms; Berit Olam:* Studies in Hebrew Narrative and Poetry (Collegeville, MN: A Michael Glassier Book published by The Liturgical Press, 2001), p. 11.

foes," rising as a mocking voice that claims God will not help... or perhaps *cannot* help. The adversaries are counted as tens of thousands; numbers too daunting to reasonably contemplate overcoming.

Yet there is a thread of promise, woven with strands of unbreakable steel and coursing right through the drawn battle lines.

> You, O Lord, are a shield around me,
> my glory, and the one who lifts my head.
> I cry aloud to the Lord,
> and he answers me from his holy hill.
> (Psalm 3:3-4)

Contrary to the taunts of the foes, God is *not* absent and *not* impotent after all. Even in the midst of profound disorientation, a sure proclamation of God's steadfastness is made. Furthermore, the proclamation is borne of experience. In spite of the presence of "tens of thousands of foes," the singer can lay down and find restful sleep. This is an audacious act of almost prophetic proportions. As Schaefer explains,

> Amidst the military assault, surrounded by innumerable
> enemies *rising up* to launch the final attack, the
> psalmist quietly *lies down* and falls asleep, and
> then awakes (v. 5). Life, with an accent on the most
> defenseless activity of resting, continues its normal
> rhythm.[49]

Anyone who has spent an anxious night tossing and turning in worry over some detail of life will appreciate just how deeply this faith in God's presence runs.

The one piece of Psalm 3 that does not quite make it into Steve's song has to do with a call for vengeance. Given the vividness of the language, it is not altogether surprising that Steve omitted this cry.

> For you strike all my enemies on the cheek:

---

[49] *ibid.*, p. 12.

you break the teeth of the wicked.
(Psalm 3:7b)

I once heard John Bell from the Iona Community remark that "the single most proscribed sin in the Bible is gossip:" bearing false witness, slander, malicious talk, and so on. You have to wonder, as Schaefer does, if what is signaled here is a cry for retribution against foes who have attacked with words. Certainly the Absalom narrative, which always stands in this psalm's background, is filled with verbal assault and game-playing (2 Samuel 15:1-6). It is beyond dispute that some of the deepest damage can be done by gossip and slander, no less now than then. Any wonder the wish for bruised faces and broken teeth is voiced?

As is true in any lament, and particularly those with hard tones of vengeance, the whole of a person's experience must be expressed. At least cathartic, and potentially the beginning of new orientation, these psalms "help people to die completely to the old situation... (and)... to say as dramatically as possible, 'That is all over now.'"[50] Needless to say, what God does with our desire to see all of those broken teeth is God's business. For our part, we must learn to land the whole works on God's plate and then dare to lie down and trustfully sleep. Frankly, I would love to see Steve do a slight rewrite of this song, working in some sense of the grittier cry for retribution. I know he's got it in him. We all do.

STEVE BELL

I'm not a strict pacifist, but I certainly lean heavily in that direction. So I was a little surprised one morning when this, of all psalms, inspired a song. Several nights after the song came, I dreamt that I was a soldier lying in a field, wounded from battle. I don't recall the nature of my wounds, but I knew I was dying, and that many of my comrades were wounded and dying around me as well. We had been ambushed by a fearsome enemy and had

---

[50] Walter Brueggemann, *Praying the Psalms,* p. 26.

taken a terrible blow. Grief was overwhelming me as I was fading in and out of consciousness, feeling like all was lost. Suddenly, I felt a hand underneath my neck; someone was helping lift me to a sitting position so I could see the aftermath of the battle. I looked around the field and realized we hadn't taken as big a hit as I had assumed. Many of my comrades were alright, and were attending to the wounded and assessing the damage. I began to cry from relief.

Then I turned my head to see who was so kindly helping me sit up, and I was staggered to see the noble face of my king, bloodied and bruised from battle. His eyes filled with loving pride as he looked across the field to see his warriors begin to rise from the smouldering chaos. And I would have happily given every limb for that single moment. It was an incredible moment of grace, and I woke up with this song in my head.

Jesus My Glory
music and lyric adaptation by Steve Bell
(based on Psalm 3, Anglo Genevan Psalter)

> Oh Lord how quickly grows
> The number of my foes
> Who wantonly oppress me
> And multiplied are they
> Who rise to my dismay
> And day by day distress me
> Though heavy my despair
> They scornfully declare
> To my humiliation
> That you, oh God, no more
> Would help me as before
> Or come to my salvation

> *But Lord you always are a shield about my heart*
> *A warrior fierce and free surrounding me*
> *In the hour of my dread you lift my weary head*
> *All trembling subsides and I cry*
> *Jesus my... my glory!*

So I lay down and slept
In peace for I am kept
By his divine protection
The Lord is at my side
My safety he supplies
Whatever my affliction
Defended by his hand
I shall undaunted stand
While thousands press around me
Though furious foemen wage
Their war with mighty rage
Yet non can ere defeat me

PSALM 19

THE HEAVENS declare the glory of God: and the firmament showeth
his handywork. One day telleth another: and one night certifieth
another. There is neither speech nor language: but their voices are heard
among them. Their sound is gone out into all lands: and their words
into the ends of the world. In them hath he set a tabernacle for the sun:
which cometh forth as a bridegroom out of his chamber, and rejoiceth
as a giant to run his course. It goeth forth from the uttermost part of the
heaven, and runneth about unto the end of it again: and there is nothing
hid from the heat thereof.

The law of the Lord is an undefiled law, converting the soul: the
testimony of the Lord is sure, and giveth wisdom unto the simple.

The statutes of the Lord are right, and rejoice the heart: the
commandment of the Lord is pure, and giveth light unto the eyes. The
fear of the Lord is clean, and endureth for ever: the judgements of the
Lord are true, and righteous altogether. More to be desired are they than
gold, yea, than much fine gold: sweeter also than honey, and the honey-
comb. Moreover, by them is thy servant taught: and in keeping of them
there is great reward.

Who can tell how oft he offendeth: O cleanse thou me from my secret
faults. Keep thy servant also from presumptuous sins, lest they get the
dominion over me: so shall I be undefiled, and innocent from
the great offence.

Let the words of my mouth, and the meditation of my heart: be always
acceptable in thy sight, O Lord: my strength, and my redeemer.

PSALM 19
PLEASING TO YOU

JAMIE HOWISON

I have heard the same story repeated countless times. Someone vows to read the entire Bible cover to cover, yet after making it through Genesis and Exodus, gets bogged down about three chapters into Leviticus. This experience is so common that several publishers have developed versions of "the Bible in a year," which take books like Leviticus and break them into manageable pieces to be read over the course of the whole year. In fact, such versions generally schedule excerpts from these rather dense—and to our eyes obscure—books alongside the more reader-friendly Gospels or similar narrative texts.

The Old Testament laws do not exactly make for riveting reading, particularly for the Christian who is less than clear as to the practical or spiritual relevance of this material. If we do slug our way through Leviticus, our most likely response is relief: relief that we made it through all twenty-seven chapters without throwing in the towel, and a deeper relief that those laws are part of the *old* covenant. After all, we quite like to have bacon with our Saturday breakfast, to say nothing of the occasional lobster tail. Free from all guilt, we add meat to our cheese pizza, wear garments made of blended fabric, and attend public worship even on a morning when we are suffering an outbreak of eczema.[51]

Read through those Old Testament laws, and it is hard to *not* feel relief that they do not bind us or dictate the details of our daily life choices. Oh, we might proof-text from the laws when it suits our purposes, but if we are honest and thoroughgoing in our reading of these texts, we will soon have to admit that if we use Leviticus 18:22 to oppose same-sex marriage then we just might have to rethink our business practices and understandings of land ownership in light of the Levitical laws on Sabbatical and Jubilee. "Thank goodness," we think, "that we can stand with the apostle Paul and say, 'we hold that a person is justified by faith apart from the works prescribed by the law' (Romans 3:28)." There are other biblical resources for reflecting on sexuality; we don't have to rearrange our church's investment portfolio in light of Jubilee; and we can have a nice seafood pasta for dinner tonight. We are most definitely a *new* covenant people.

Of course, this interpretation is all too simplistic, doing service neither to *torah* nor to Christian proclamation. After all, in the same epistle Paul rhetorically asks his reader, "Do we then overthrow the law by this faith?" Before we can even begin to form an answer, he replies, "By no means! On the contrary, we uphold the law" (Romans 3:31).

"I believe there's more to this than we're getting," writes Steve, which is probably one of the more helpful statements a Christian poet could make in response to the law. Psalm 19 is a song written in thanks and celebration for *torah*. The psalm has two

---

[51] In *Harper's Bible Dictionary,* 'Leprosy' is defined as follows: "In the OT a disorder affecting humans, fabrics, and houses. There are different types of leprosy that afflict persons (Lev. 13). Though it is not clear what these skin diseases are, it is certain that they are not modern leprosy (Hansen's disease). The plague in fabrics and houses is described as greenish or reddish spots (Lev. 13:49; 14:37), thus indicating a type of mold or mildew." Paul J. Achtemeier, ed. *Harper's Bible Dictionary* (San Francisco: Harper & Row, Publishers, 1985), p. 555. There is some serious speculation that the term was sufficiently broad to include conditions such as eczema and psoriasis.

sections: verses 1-6, which focus on creation and the splendor of the sun; and verses 7-14, which focus on the law's role in giving boundaries to human will and desire. As the English theologian Oliver O'Donovan has shown, the two sections are inextricably entwined.[52] The material on creation points to the Creator, who in creating has wrought something splendid, unique, ordered and life-giving. Throughout these six verses, the sun is given particular emphasis as a source of life and energy.

O'Donovan then suggests that the introduction of the theme of law—of *torah*—right on the heels of this image of the sun is far from incidental. The *torah is* analogous to the sun, in that it too is all about direction, light and purpose. *Torah* gives life and energy, and is set out in accordance with the divine plan. We encounter the *torah* in the same way in which we encounter God's creation and sun—as always, already there. The task, according to this psalmist, is to begin to take notice and live accordingly.

"I believe there's something good here to ponder," writes Steve, and surely there is. To "ponder" is to hear, reflect, deliberate, and decide. It is *not* to wallop ourselves or our neighbours with a selected legalistic club when it supports our theology, and to happily pack the rest of the clubs in the "old covenant" closet when they don't suit us.

It is useful to remind ourselves that *torah* is not simply or narrowly *laws*. *Torah*, or the five books of Moses, includes our birth narrative as the people of God. From the proto-history of Genesis 1-11 through the stories of the patriarchs and matriarchs to the Exodus and wilderness wanderings, *torah* tells us where we have come from and to whom we belong. *Torah* tells of how a new people, an alternative people, was carved out by God, and how things so basic as pots and pans and property lines were crucial details in that formation. *Torah* calls us to pay attention to both the mundane and the splendid, and to find in that "attending" an alternative social identity.

---

[52] Oliver O'Donovan, *Law and Judgement*, a lecture delivered at Wycliffe College, Toronto, May 15, 2002.

Allow me to indulge in a bit of reflective pondering. Deuteronomy 17:14-20 sets out the terms under which kingship might be incorporated into Israel's political life. The passage begins with a set of conditions. A king for Israel must be an Israelite, and must not acquire vast herds of horses, rooms full of wives, or large reserves of gold and silver. In other words, there are limits placed on might and power, sexual license, and wealth... and at this point the usual cast of royal-candidates should quietly bow out of the running. So what is a king supposed to do and be? One who sits on the seat of authority and reads *torah*. Whatever judgements the king makes are to be borne of *that* grounding and *that* pondering.

Can you imagine if a king had succeeding in living that vision? Perhaps Josiah came closest, but most of the other kings of Israel fell prey to power, sex, wealth, or some combination of the three. More provocatively, what if we used this text as a way to rethink the ministry of ordained leaders in our churches? Power, sex, and money are temptations that continue to unseat people in ministry. In some cases, we may even be building power and wealth right into the very fabric of the job-description. The pastor as CEO of the congregation; financial remuneration as the indicator of personal and professional worth; endowing leaders with personal power not borne of any real spiritual authority; these are just a few of the traps visible just below the surface in some places within our church culture. How might things be different in our churches if we imagined that a pastor's primary role was to sit on the chair of authority—*authority*, not power—and read scripture?

If this question begins a conversation about the nature of leadership and authority, then we are doing precisely what the psalmist says we will do when we begin to take notice of *torah*. Yes, as Christians *torah* is read in light of gospel claims, but we must not try to read gospel without also steeping ourselves in *torah*. This is the claim Psalm 19 places on the imagination of Christians: that there are things we are not quite getting; things that we still need to ponder; things, too, that time will show need no defending.

STEVE BELL

For several years we lived in the country, just outside Winnipeg, on a peaceful acreage rimmed by birch and oak forest. We built a home there, with large windows so we could watch the whirling birds, see the gentle deer, and catch an occasional glimpse of the splendid red fox that would sometimes trot across our lawn. One morning I was sitting by the east window as the sun was just beginning to rise. As it appeared on the horizon, I was suddenly overwhelmed by the reliability of its rising and an awareness of the good it accomplishes every day. My Bible happened to be flopped open in my lap and I looked down to see Psalm 19. This song soon followed.

Pleasing To You
music and lyric adaptation by Steve Bell

> The sun comes about
> With a force and a strength
> Bursting out from the ground
> Like a hound to the race
> It's the same every day after day
> Unto ages unending
> I believe there's more to this than were getting
>
> It again rose today
> As I've come to expect
> Like the bridegroom awakes
> From his honeymoon bed
> To the one that he loves
> And the object of all he can offer
> I believe there's something good here to ponder
>
> *The law of the Lord is right*
> *A blazing light*
> *Ever making wise the simple*
> *The wisdom of God is whole*
> *Restoring the soul*
> *And the honour of His people*

What can gold mean to my heart
When much sweeter fare by far
Is the counsel of the Holy One
My rock and my redeemer and my God

The heavens proclaim
What I'm trying to say
Night after night
And day after day
There's no time and no place
No speech where the truth is suspending
I believe that some things need no defending

May the words of my mouth
And the thoughts of my heart
Be pleasing to you
Be pleasing to you my God
My God

PSALM 8

O LORD our Governor, how excellent is thy Name in all the world: thou
that hast set thy glory above the heavens! Out of the mouth of very babes
and sucklings hast thou ordained strength, because of thine enemies:
that thou mightest still the enemy and the avenger.

For I will consider thy heavens, even the works of thy fingers: the
moon and the stars, which thou hast ordained. What is man, that thou
art mindful of him: and the son of man, that thou visitest him? Thou
madest him lower than the angels: to crown him with glory and worship.
Thou makest him to have dominion of the works of thy hands: and thou
hast put all things in subjection under his feet;
All sheep and oxen: yea, and the beasts of the field; The fowls of the air,
and the fishes of the sea: and whatsoever walketh through the paths of
the seas. O Lord our Governor: how excellent is thy
Name in all the world!

PSALM 8 & HEBREWS 1
OH LOVE

JAMIE HOWISON

There is always a risk when we read the Bible that we will allow ourselves to get stuck on *this* verse, *this* chapter, *this* parable, as being *the* meaning of scripture or faith or life. We imagine that it all comes down to a particular passage, and then we proceed to measure everything else against our particular reading of it. Think of the guy who used to hold up the sign reading "John 3:16" at all of those televised sporting events, convinced that if the atheists and agnostics in TV Land would only read that one verse their lives would be changed. It is true that Martin Luther believed John 3:16 to be the "gospel in miniature," but Luther could reach that conclusion because he knew the entire Bible so intimately.

I know of no better antidote to such an approach to scripture than Robert Farrar Capon's image of the "Bible as movie." The Bible, says Capon, is the Film assembled by the master Director—the Holy Spirit—from this wild range of often quite raw material. The Director, refusing to let anything land on the cutting room floor, has pieced together a masterly, complex, and far-ranging film that must be watched again and again and again. According to Capon,

"It is like watching a foreign film with no subtitles." Every time you think you have it all figured out, something new enters the screen and throws all of your neat conclusions out of whack. *And* you have to watch the whole film. You cannot push the "pause" button on the DVD player and say, "ah, that's what the Bible means," because that compromises the Director's key artistic decision, which is to work with multiple voices, intertwined images, and overlapping perspectives and story-lines.[53]

Were you to read Psalm 8 as a self-contained and independent theological proclamation, you would gain a very particular vision of God, creation and humanity. A good and truthful vision, mind you, but a very particular one all the same.

Walter Brueggemann counts this psalm amongst the "psalms of safe orientation." A creation song—which for the people of Israel always meant a song pointing beyond creation to the Creator—it arises from a place of spiritual confidence and stability, in which life is experienced as "reliable, equitable, and generous."[54] In this view,

> The world is God's way of bestowing blessing upon us.
> Our times are ordered by God according to the seasons
> of the year, according to the seasons of life, according
> to the needs of the day. In all of these processes, we find
> ourselves to be safe and free; we know that out of no
> great religious insight, but because that is the way life
> comes to us.[55]

"That is the way life comes to us." Perhaps not always or everywhere, but we have all had those moments that resonate with what the psalmist describes. As you watch the sun set over the lake during your summer vacation, or as you look at the tiny hands of a new-

---

[53] I was first introduced to the "Bible as film" approach during conversations with Robert in the autumn of 2000. For a detailed application of the model, see his *Genesis: the Movie* (Grand Rapids, Michigan: William B. Eerdmans Publishing Company, 2003).

[54] Walter Brueggemann, *Spirituality of the Psalms* (Minneapolis: Fortress Press, 2002), p. 22.

[55] *Ibid.*, p.22.

born child, or as you and your beloved finish that great gourmet meal celebrating some milestone in your life together... all is well in the great God's universe.

But because we are students of the Film, we keep watching and eventually come to Hebrews 1. It is a good thing that we are students of a film made by this particular Director, because in the real world those experiences of safe orientation do not last. Vacations end, babies get colic, marriages get into trouble... and "the whole creation has been groaning in labour pains until now" (Romans 8:22).

Before the creation, says the writer of Hebrews, was the Son, "through whom God created the world" (Hebrews 1:2c). "He is the reflection of God's glory and the exact imprint of God's very being, and he sustains all things by his powerful word" (Hebrews 1:3a). Where Psalm 8 had invited us to see how creation points to the Creator, Hebrews 1 calls us to see Christ as being *the* reflection and imprint of God. Creation is an indicator and an icon of the divine; but like all icons and images, it has a limited shelf life. Christ alone is the lasting and exact imprint of God's being. Under the inspiration of the Director, the writer quotes Psalm 102:25-27, using it as a proclamation about Christ:

> And,
> 'In the beginning, Lord, you founded the earth,
> and the heavens are the work of your hands;
> they will perish, but you remain;
> they will all wear out like clothing;
> like a cloak you will roll them up,
> and like clothing they will be changed.
> But you are the same,
> and your years will never end.'
> (Hebrews 1:10-12)

And so the created order, both earth and heavens, will pass away. Majestic and safe and secure as it all can seem, creation is instead transient, and points to a Creator whose being is *not* exhausted by, or limited to, the created work. Christ, the Son, is the only one named here as co-eternal.

Still, you need to keep watching the Film. The song "Oh Love" draws on not only Psalm 8 and Hebrews 1, but also on Steve's deeper immersion in the Director's great project. Steve knows the film, and so proclaims how in and through the co-eternal Son, God has invited even us—"what are human beings that you are mindful of them?" (Psalm 8:4a)—to have a share in the inheritance. With this understanding, the final verse of the song becomes a deep prayer for a humanity that so often doesn't "get it."

> But few long for
> An end to the fuss
> And clamouring din
> Managing mess
> Instead of fundamentally living on trust
> Encouraging love
> As the day approaches near
> And our time is ended here.

Now, go watch the film again.

STEVE BELL

I love to read in the morning. I'll often wake up early and read for several hours before anyone else in the house stirs. One day, in the middle of recording the *Waiting for Aidan* album, I woke up unusually late, which didn't leave much time before I was expected at the studio. I only had a few minutes on the couch before heading out to work, and so I chose the daily lectionary reading in which the first chapter of Hebrews riffs on Psalm 8. Suddenly a song came rushing down the pike so quickly that it was complete in about half an hour. Songs rarely come that rapidly, but it is always rather exhilarating when they do. I got to the studio on time, taught my band members the song, and recorded it the same day it was written.

I remember the passage—and the song it inspired—elevating my spirit to astonished wonder as I considered the gaping chasm between the glory of God and humanity's relentless, damaging ego-centrism. Two days later, the twin towers of 9/11 came down, and this song became my steadying companion as we all staggered under the weight of those days.

Oh Love
music and lyric adaptation by Steve Bell

You, Master, started it all
Laid the foundation
Fashioned the stars
But the earth and the skies
Will one day wear out
Like a worn-out old coat
But not you, you stay the same
Never fade and never change

It's true faster and faster we fall
In a sickening spin
We're tumbling carelessly
And voluntarily making it all
Appear like the dream of our choosing faculty
We're so proud to be so free

Oh Love, what are you thinking of
How could it be true that you are mindful of us
All day I've been thinking this way
Passing the time
Sounding the name
That is echoing over the earth

You hover over the earth
Scattering hope for,
gathering fuel for a raging good fire
A beacon of truth
No more reproduced on a page or chiseled stone
Now the heart is written on

But few long for an end to the fuss
And clamouring din
We're managing mess
Instead of fundamentally living on trust
Encouraging love as the day approaches near
And our time is ended here

PSALM 116

I AM well pleased: that the Lord hath heard the voice of my prayer; That he hath inclined his ear unto me: therefore will I call upon him as long as I live. The snares of death compassed me round about: and the pains of hell got hold upon me. I shall find trouble and heaviness, and I will call upon the Name of the Lord: O Lord, I beseech thee, deliver my soul.

Gracious is the Lord, and righteous: yea, our God is merciful. The Lord preserveth the simple: I was in misery, and he helped me. Turn again then unto thy rest, O my soul: for the Lord hath rewarded thee.

And why? thou hast delivered my soul from death: mine eyes from tears, and my feet from falling. I will walk before the Lord: in the land of the living. I believed, and therefore will I speak; but I was sore troubled: I said in my haste, All men are liars.

What reward shall I give unto the Lord: for all the benefits that he hath done unto me? I will receive the cup of salvation: and call upon the Name of the Lord. I will pay my vows now in the presence of all his people: right dear in the sight of the Lord is the death of his saints. Behold, O Lord, how that I am thy servant: I am thy servant, and the son of thine handmaid; thou hast broken my bonds in sunder. I will offer to thee the sacrifice of thanksgiving: and will call upon the Name of the Lord. I will pay my vows unto the Lord, in the sight of all his people: in the courts of the Lord's house, even in the midst of thee, O Jerusalem.

Praise the Lord.

PSALM 116

JAMIE HOWISON

For Steve's lyrics to this Psalm, he uses a modest adaptation of Psalm 116 from the "Anglo-Genevan Psalter." A fairly recent product of the English-speaking Christian Reformed tradition— *The Book of Praise,* of which the Psalter is a key part, was published in the early 1970s— the roots of this particular Psalter go deep into the heart of the Reformation.

The key figure behind the original French "Genevan Psalter" of 1562 was John Calvin himself. Calvin was convinced that worship belonged to the whole people—to the *laos*—and not primarily to the ordained clergy. Accordingly, the Genevan Psalter was designed to be sung by congregations, with the Psalms set in metrical form to singable tunes.

I suspect Calvin would have been pleased to see how this psalm has been taken, through CD and concert appearances, even further afield than just the average Sunday congregation. He might have flinched to see a couple of the original stanzas omitted, but may well have softened on this point once he heard how the psalm has spoken to Steve in the context of his daughter Sarah's survival of an eating disorder. Even the tough and uncompromising reformer Calvin would have heard what Steve manages to say *through* these words.

The original Hebrew psalm is quite likely a song of thanksgiving for recovery from an illness. As you read a more conventional and non-metrical translation such as the New Revised Standard Version, you can't help but hear the sense of relief and deep gratitude in the psalmist's voice:

> I love the Lord, because he has heard
> my voice and my supplications.
> Because he inclined his ear to me,
> therefore I will call on him as long as I live.
> The snares of death encompassed me;
> the pangs of Sheol laid hold on me;
> I suffered distress and anguish.
> Then I called on the name of the Lord:
> O Lord, I pray, save my life!'
> Gracious is the Lord, and righteous;
> our God is merciful.
> (Psalm 116:1-5)

Thankful, too, that in the midst of the crisis, faith managed to hold:

> I kept my faith, even when I said,
> 'I am greatly afflicted;'
> I said in my consternation,
> 'Everyone is a liar.'
> (Psalm 116:10-11)

Everyone is a liar? But who is this "everyone?" Those who said "there is no God," or "God isn't much interested in this," or "repent of whatever sin you've committed and *then* talk about healing." "Everyone," in short, who doubted both the love and power of God, and the fidelity or worth of the person who prays. Those, too, who said, "do such-and-such, and God will be bound to give you such-and-such." What this psalmist has discovered is a kind of deep patience, echoed in the words of the novelist Reynolds Price:

> [We embrace] the mysterious will of a God whom we
> must believe, in the long run, to be loving. And the long
> run can be very long indeed.[56]

I suspect this patience is the hardest thing for us. It must have
been for Steve and his wife Nanci, as they waited out Sarah's
eating disorder over a two-year period before being able to voice
words of gratitude through this psalm. Certainly it is the same
for the cancer patient, or the friend or lover of the cancer patient,
sitting in the palliative care ward wondering when the promise
of healing might begin. Indeed it is the same for all of us, in the
various shipwrecks of our own lives, waiting to see and feel and
know how resurrection will transform us from partial, fallen, and
compromised creatures into something closer to the fullness of
life hinted at in our scriptures.

The thing about Psalm 116 is its remarkable absence of shallow
triumphalism. I just don't picture a dashing multi-millionaire as
the author of such words.

> The Lord protects the simple;
> when I was brought low, he saved me.
> Return, O my soul, to your rest,
> for the Lord has dealt bountifully with you.
> (Psalm 116:6-7)

"Return, O my soul, to your rest." Simplicity, balance, perspective,
and a kind of resolve seep from these words. Saved not from the
shipwreck, but in the very midst of it. And of course, that is what
the gospel is ultimately about, isn't it?

---

[56] Reynolds Price, *A Serious Way of Wondering* (New York: Scribner, 2003)
p. 128.

STEVE BELL

One evening, when my daughter Sarah was about 14 years old, she came into our bedroom and, with many tears, confessed how she had been suffering with an eating disorder for some time, and that she now feared it was getting dangerous. Just weeks before, I had sung at a funeral for a young woman who wasn't able to pull out of a similar disorder. My heart was wrenched to think of our precious daughter suffering such inner turmoil and perilous circumstance.

To make a long story short, we got help for Sarah and she worked hard at recovery. It took a couple of years, but there came a point when I began to believe she might fully recover. One morning in particular I realized the danger had truly passed, and of course grateful tears flowed, as did this song:

Psalm 116
music and lyric adaptation by Steve Bell
(adapted from the Anglo-Genevan Psalter)

> I love the Lord the fount of life and grace
> He heard my voice, my cry, my supplication
> Inclined his year, gave strength and consolation
> In life, in death, I'll always seek his face
>
> The cords of death held me in deep despair
> The terrors of the grave caused me to languish
> I suffered untold grief and bitter anguish
> In my distress I turned to God in prayer
>
> I cried to him, oh I beseech thee Lord
> Preserve her life and prove thyself my Saviour
> The Lord is just and he shows grace and favour
> In boundless mercy he fulfills his word

The Lord preserves the helpless graciously
For when brought low in him I found salvation
Come now, my soul, relieved from tribulation
Return to rest, the Lord has favoured thee

What shall I render to my Saviour now
For all the riches of his consolation
With joy I'll take the cup of his salvation
And call upon his name with thankful vow

Jerusalem, within your walls I'll praise
The Lord's great name, and with a spirit lowly
I'll pay all my vows, oh Zion fair and holy
Come join with me and bless him all your days

This prince of thine, oh Zion, fair and holy
Come join with me and bless him all your days

PSALM 70

HASTE THEE, O God, to deliver me; make haste to help me, O Lord. Let them be ashamed and confounded that seek after my soul; let them be turned backward and put to confusion that wish me evil. Let them for their reward be soon brought to shame, that cry over me, There! there!

But let all those that seek thee be joyful and glad in thee, and let all such as delight in thy salvation say always, The Lord be praised. As for me, I am poor and in misery; haste thee unto me, O God. Thou art my helper, and my redeemer; O Lord, make no long tarrying.

POSTSCRIPT
PSALM 70:1
COME TO MY HELP OH GOD

STEVE BELL

The late addition of this final chapter comes as I flex a little executive muscle to include one last psalm-song and reflection, dedicating it to Jamie Howison, my dear co-belligerent, who has been a great spiritual friend and mentor for most of my adult life. It was Jamie who did most of the heavy lifting for this book. His vision has propelled it from the beginning, and it has been his encouragement to me over the years that has helped me to trust the gifts I've been entrusted with, fortifying me with confidence to soldier on through the more difficult and disorienting days which every sojourner will inevitably face.

So... one last psalm and one final song:

Come to my help oh God. Lord hurry to my rescue. Psalm 70:1

St. John Cassian (CE 360-435) instructed his followers that this one little verse contained all that was needed for the fullness of prayer. Praying this verse was sufficient to ward off "worldly disturbances" and the "turbulence of sin" until the "union of the Father and Son, of

Son and Father...fill[ed] our senses and our minds."[57]
Recalling the words of his elder, Brother Isaac, who encouraged continuous repetition of this one verse, Cassian's writings reveal how the earliest monastics used this simple device to learn how to pray unceasingly. He describes how this verse carries within it a cry of help to God in the face of every danger. It expresses the humility of a pious confession. It conveys the watchfulness borne of unending worry and fear. It conveys a sense of our frailty, the assurance of being heard, the confidence in help that is always and everywhere present."[58]

The elder monk warned, however, that spiritual danger lay not only in times of distress and temptation, but equally in seasons of joy and good fortune. The early saints were well aware that the evil one could distort the good even as Christ could redeem the bad. And so there is no circumstance where this humble prayer is not needed.

I am reminded of Rudyard Kipling's famous poem "If" where he suggests that spiritual maturity comes "...*if* you can meet with Triumph and Disaster, and treat those two imposters just the same..."[59] One hears the echoes of antiquity in these lines.

Last summer, I co-led a course on contemplative prayer with Bruce Hindmarsh at Regent College, which is situated on the beautiful UBC campus in Vancouver. Bruce was the heavy lifter of the course—much the same as Jamie is for this book—and I provided the occasional anecdote along with whatever music seemed appropriate. I wrote this simple, repetitious song as a prayer we could sing daily together at the beginning and end of sessions. Mindful of the ancient suspicion of both triumph and disaster, I wrote the melody to alternate between major and minor keys, to help trace the petition over every experience, and beseech Christ to redeem and sanctify the fullness of our daily lives. We sang it in Taizé style, repeating it over and over as we sank into the prayer and

---

[57] John Cassian, "Conference Ten," in *Conferences* (New York: Paulist Press, 1985), p. 128-129

[58] Cassian, "Conference Ten," p. 133

[59] Rudyard Kipling, "If—" accessed March 18, 2015 through "Academy of American Poets," http://www.poets.org/poetsorg/poem/if%E2%80%94

let it seep into our pores. I now find I sing it many times a day—often unconsciously—sometimes as I go to sleep, and sometimes waking to find my heart already singing it. It seems a fitting end to this book and the accompanying CD.

It has been good for me to go back over this collection of psalm-songs—to recall whatever anxieties or elevations of spirit that prompted them, and to read Jamie's reflections. If I were to start over with my current collection of experiences, I realize that I'd probably write very different songs. But this is the beauty of these ancient prayer-poems—they are evergreen and on-the-ready to express the deepest longings of the human heart, sung for a God who cares to hear.

Thanks for reading. Thanks for listening. Peace to you and yours.

WORKS CITED

Bonhoeffer, Dietrich. *Letters and Papers from Prison*. New York: Touchstone, 1997.

Bono, "Introduction," *The Pocket Canon Psalms*. New York: Grove Press, 1999.

Brueggemann, Walter. *Spirituality of the Psalms*. Minneapolis: Fortress, 2002.

_____. *Praying the Psalms*. Winona, Minnesota: Saint Mary's Press, Christian Brothers Publications, 1993.

Capon, Robert Farrar. *Genesis: the Movie*. Grand Rapids: William B. Eerdmans Publishing Company, 2003.

_____. *Health, Money & Love... and why we don't enjoy them*. Grand Rapids: William B. Eerdmans Publishing Company, 1990.

Cullmann, Oscar. *Immortality of the Soul or Resurrection of the Dead?* London: The Epworth Press, 1958.

Hauerwas, Stanley. "Punishing Christians." In Hauerwas, *Performing the Faith*. Grand Rapids: Brazos Press, 2004.

Limburg, James. *Psalms*. Louisville, KY: Westminster John Knox Press, 2000.

Norris, Kathleen. *The Psalms*. New York: Riverhead Books, 1997.

Price, Reynolds. *A Serious Way of Wondering*. New York: Scribner, 2003.

Schaefer, Konrad OSB. *Psalms; Berit Olam: Studies in Hebrew Narrative and Poetry*. Collegeville, MN: The Liturgical Press, A Michael Glazier Book, 2001.

Toombs, Lawrence E. "The Psalms." In *The Interpreter's One-Volume Commentary on the Bible*, edited by Charles M. Laymon. Nashville: Abingdon Press, 1971.

Updike, John. "Transaction." In Updike, *Problems and other stories*. New York: Fawcett Crest, 1981.

Weiser, Artur. *The Psalms*. Philadelphia: The Westminster Press, 1962.

Tanner, Beth LaNeel. "How Long, O Lord! Will Your People Suffer in Silence Forever?" In *Psalms and Practice*, edited by Stephen Breck Reid. Collegeville, MN: The Liturgical Press, A Michael Glazier Book, 2001.

ABOUT THE AUTHORS

Jamie Howison is a priest of the Anglican Church of Canada, the founding pastoral leader of saint benedict's table, and the author of *God's Mind in that Music: Theological Explorations through the Music of John Coltrane.*

www.stbenedictstable.ca

Steve Bell is a Canadian prairie singer-songwriter and founder of Signpost Music, whose career has yielded 18 CDs of music and concert appearances world-over. Increasingly in demand as a conference and campus speaker, Steve has also recently co-authored *Pilgrim Year,* an online multimedia collection of reflections based on the Christian calendar year (www.pilgrimyear.com).

www.stevebell.com